C0-ADL-085

MUSEUMS COUNT

MUSEUMS
COUNT

A REPORT BY
_____

THE AMERICAN ASSOCIATION OF MUSEUMS
_____

WASHINGTON, D.C.
_____

MUSEUMS COUNT
A Report by the American Association of Museums

Project Writer/Editor: Ann Hofstra Grogg
AAM Editors: Susannah Cassedy O'Donnell, Donald Garfield
Art Direction: Polly Franchine
Design concept courtesy of Philip Morris Companies Inc.
Printed by Schneidereith and Sons, Inc., Baltimore, Maryland.

Title page photo: *Fernbank Museum of Natural History, Atlanta, Georgia. Photograph by Jonathan Hillyer.*

Published by the American Association of Museums.
© 1994, the American Association of Museums.
All rights reserved. No part of this book may be reproduced in any format, with the exception of brief quotes in the context of a critical review, without prior written permission from the publisher.

American Association of Museums
1225 Eye St. NW
Suite 200
Washington, D.C. 20005
202/289–1818

Library of Congress Cataloging-in-Publication Data
Museums count / [by the American Association of Museums; project editor, Ann Grogg].
            p. cm.
        Includes index.
        ISBN 0-931201-17-9 : $30.00
        1. Museums—United States. 2. Museums—United States—Statistics.
    I. Grogg, Ann. II. American Association of Museums
    AM11.M73 1994
    069'.0973—dc20

                                        93-51504
                                        CIP

648 73

CONTENTS

LIST OF CHARTS AND GRAPHS

FOREWORD

P HILIP MORRIS COMPANIES INC. is proud to sponsor the American Association of Museums' National Museum Survey and *Museums Count*. This report is a study of American museums ranging from major visual arts institutions to historic sites to zoos. It contains information that is important to everyone involved in the museum field.

Research on museums and their economic impact is relatively rare, due to limited resources. However, the American Association of Museums has completed the most expansive museum study in over 10 years. This survey will contribute to current reflection on the field that is necessary to help ensure the long-term survival of these institutions.

Philip Morris Companies Inc. salutes the American Association of Museums and its dedication to preserving the history and strengthening the future of all museums in America.

Stephanie French

Stephanie French
Vice President, Corporate Contributions and Cultural Affairs
Philip Morris Companies Inc.

ACKNOWLEDGMENTS

MANY INDIVIDUALS PROVIDED HELP IN CREATING THIS BOOK. The origins for it are found in the 1992 publication by the American Association of Museums, the *Data Report from the 1989 National Museum Survey,* the most extensive survey of its kind. Thanks is due to the hundreds of museum professionals across the country who responded to AAM's request for the data that formed the basis of the survey. The senior museum professionals who served on AAM's Data Collection Steering Committee also provided guidance and expertise, as well as many hours of their valuable time. Their names and affiliations are listed on page 13 of this book.

We wish to thank the funders of the survey: the Institute of Museum Services, the National Endowment for the Arts, the National Endowment for the Humanities, the National Science Foundation, The Rockefeller Foundation, The Dillon Fund, The Max and Victoria Dreyfus Foundation Inc., James G. Hanes Memorial Fund/Foundation, and the Bureau of National Affairs.

Philip Morris Companies Inc., the data collection survey's corporate sponsor, deserves a special thanks for funding the survey and its related publications. In addition, a generous grant from Philip Morris Companies Inc. made the printing of *Museums Count* possible.

A special thanks is also due to James Blackaby, museum consultant and member of AAM's Data Collection Steering Committee, for his help in interpreting the data that are the basis for this book, and to Ann Hofstra Grogg, the project writer/editor, for her diligent efforts at rendering the complex accessible.

John Strand
Director of Publications
American Association of Museums

DATA COLLECTION NATIONAL STEERING COMMITTEE

Co-chairs

Dan L. Monroe, executive director, Peabody & Essex Museum, Salem, Mass.

Michael Spock, vice president for public programs, Field Museum of Natural History, Chicago

Members

Sarah Becker, acting director, Stabler-Leadbeater, Apothecary Museum, Alexandria, Va., and consultant to nonprofit organizations

James Blackaby, museum consultant, formerly curator of Mercer and Fonthill Museums, Bucks County Historical Society, Doylestown, Pa.

Barbara Butler, program director, National Science Foundation

Rebecca Danvers, program director, Institute of Museum Services

Bruce Evans, director, Mint Museum of Art, Charlotte, N.C.

Gail Harrity, deputy director for finance and administration, Guggenheim Museum, New York, N.Y.

Harold Horowitz, architect

Warren Iliff, director, Phoenix Zoo, Phoenix, Ariz.

Cheryl McClenney-Brooker, vice president for external affairs, Philadelphia Museum of Art

Carol Nelson, museum consultant, formerly executive director, Louisiana Association of Museums

Andrew Oliver, director, Museum Program, National Endowment for the Arts

Marsha Semmel, assistant director, Museums and Historical Organizations, National Endowment for the Humanities

Raymond H. Thompson, director, Arizona State Museum, University of Arizona, Tuscon

Dennis Wint, president, St. Louis Science Center

Program Staff: American Association of Museums

Kathy Dwyer Southern, deputy executive director, programs and policy, 1986-90

Donald A. Moore, deputy executive director, programs and policy, 1990-91

Patricia E. Williams, deputy executive director, programs and policy

Kim Igoe, director, Accreditation and Museum Standards

Alma Gates, executive assistant

Program Staff: Project Manager

Monnie Peters, consultant in survey research and long-range planning for nonprofit organizations

MUSEUMS COUNT

1

INTRODUCTION

AMERICA'S MUSEUMS ARE POPULAR PLACES. THOUSANDS OF THEM, located in every region and in almost every community throughout the country, attract hundreds of millions of visitors each year. Hundreds of thousands of individuals volunteer their time and talents to serve them. More than one hundred thousand people find their life's work in them. Museum collections include hundreds of millions of objects. Museums care for millions of acres of land and hundreds of millions of square feet of interior space. Their budgets total billions of dollars. Museums count.

Museums also count in ways that cannot be quantified. As stewards of our natural and cultural heritage, they preserve the collective natural and human experience. As educational institutions, they study and interpret that heritage, and they enlighten and enrich each visitor. They stimulate curiosity, increase knowledge, give pleasure. They acquaint us with the unfamiliar and provide new perspectives on the known. Museums continue to be established and their audiences continue to grow because, as institutions, they reflect and speak to the needs of our diverse and democratic society. They also speak to us as individuals, as participants in communities and cultures, as partners in our natural world.

Museums also count in ways that cannot be quantified. As stewards of our natural and cultural heritage, they preserve the collective natural and human experience

The United States museum community, like the United States itself, is remarkably diverse. That is one reason that quantification, even of the quantifiable, has not been easy. In type, museums run the gamut from art to zoo. Their focus might be on art, history, or science, or all three. Their collections include historic buildings, scientific instruments, furnishings, tools, paintings, sculpture, archeological remains, rocks, living plants, and animals. Some museums do not own collections but use objects and hands-on experiences to promote understanding, especially of art, nature, or technology and scientific principles. The annual budgets of museums range from a few thousand dollars to a hundred million. Their staffs range from a few part-time volunteers to hundreds of specialists. They might be a private non-profit organization, a government agency, a corporate entity, or a university affiliate.

These many institutions share common goals, however: to collect and preserve material culture and natural history, and to interpret and exhibit this heritage to the public. They also share a common mandate: to hold their collections, resources, and ideas in public trust for both present and future generations.

Left: Old Presbyterian Meeting House, Alexandria, Virginia.

Courtesy of Alexandria Convention and Visitors Bureau.

Data Stratification

Regions
The 6 regions represented by regional museum associations–

New England:
Connecticut, Maine, Massachusetts, New Hampshire, Rhode Island, Vermont

Mid-Atlantic:
District of Columbia, Delaware, Maryland, New York, New Jersey, Pennsylvania, Puerto Rico, Virgin Islands

Southeastern:
Alabama, Arkansas, Florida, Georgia, Kentucky, Louisiana, Mississippi, North Carolina, South Carolina, Tennessee, Virginia, West Virginia

Midwest:
Illinois, Indiana, Iowa, Michigan, Minnesota, Missouri, Ohio, Wisconsin

Mountain/Plains:
Colorado, Kansas, Montana, Nebraska, New Mexico, North Dakota, South Dakota, Oklahoma, Texas, Wyoming

Western:
Alaska, Arizona, California, Hawaii, Idaho, Nevada, Oregon, Utah, Washington, American Samoa, Guam

The 1989 National Museum Survey is the most extensive survey of museums ever undertaken in the United States. It was conducted by the American Association of Museums with support assistance from the Institute of Museum Services, National Endowment for the Arts, National Endowment for the Humanities, National Science Foundation, and other foundations and funding agencies. Its immediate impetus was AAM's landmark report, *Museums for a New Century*, published in 1984. The Commission on Museums for a New Century, which produced the report, felt its work had been impeded by the "lack of information about museums and the museum profession." "There are no reliable data," the commission reported, "on the characteristics of the museum work force, the availability of various kinds of public programming or the financial picture of American museums. We cannot compare organizational structures, nor do we know the extent of the development of policies in such areas as collections management. Even such simple information as the number, type, budget size, and regional distribution of museums is not regularly maintained." To meet the need for information, the commission recommended that the museum community set up "a permanent mechanism for collecting, analyzing and disseminating data about museums—their numbers and locations, their facilities and finances, their personnel and trustees, their activities and attendance."

In response, the American Association of Museums initiated the data collection project in the fall of 1987 by establishing the Data Collection National Steering Committee. Appointed by the AAM president, its members included professionals from the museum community; representatives of the federal agencies funding the project; experts in data, research, and the economics of arts and cultural organizations; and senior AAM personnel. The primary goal of the project was to produce an accurate and reliable survey of data useful to the museum community and others. An initial task was to develop a common vocabulary that would increase each museum's ability to describe and compare itself to similar institutions and increase AAM's ability to collect, organize, and disseminate this type of information. The survey was seen as a first step in a continuing data collection program that would assist museums in responding to a broader community agenda and in influencing federal, state, and regional policy making.

The Steering Committee identified as the survey's target population every institution in the United States and its territories that:
  • *is organized as a public or private nonprofit institution, existing on a permanent basis for essentially educational and aesthetic purposes*

Data Stratification

Type
The 13 disciplines identified on the Institute of Museum Services' grant applications–

   aquarium

   arboretum/botanical garden

   art museum/center

   children/youth museum

   general museum (two or more disciplines equally applicable)

   historic house/site

   history museum

   natural history or anthropology museum/site

   nature center

   planetarium

   science/technology center/museum

   specialized (a single distinct subject, or for which no other category is appropriate)

   zoo

• cares for and owns or uses tangible objects, whether animate or inanimate, and exhibits these on a regular basis

• has at least one professional staff member or the full-time equivalent, whether paid or unpaid, whose primary responsibility is the acquisition, care, or exhibition of objects owned or used by the museum

• is open to the general public on a regular basis (the general public can or may arrange to visit on at least 120 days per year).

This definition of a museum is similar to the definitions used currently by the American Association of Museums and the Institute of Museum Services. Because it was used in IMS's 1979 Museum Program Survey, the last major survey of U.S. museums, it allows for some general comparison of data for museums over a 10-year period.

The Steering Committee wanted not only to produce a general profile of American museums similar to that produced in the 1979 survey but to go beyond profile data to examine areas of concern to the American museum community and American society at large, including museum administration, collections and research, public activities, and finances. Ultimately each of these areas was addressed by a section of the questionnaire and so reported in the findings. The *Data Report from the 1989 National Museum Survey*, with more than 160 tables and graphs presenting selected findings, is available from the AAM Bookstore, 202/289-9127.

The sampling techniques used to survey the museum community are described in full in the *Data Report*. Briefly, more than 2,000 questionnaries were sent to a random selection of institutions within categories that ensured the sample would be representative. These categories were region of the country, type of museum, and budget size of museum. *Region of museum* was defined as the six U.S. regions represented by the AAM's affiliate regional museum associations. *Type of museum* was self-reported according to the 13 disciplines used by the Institute of Museum Services. *Size of museum* was determined by operating budget adjusted for museum type to accommodate differing operational requirements: a "small" aquarium, for example, might have about the same operating budget as a "large" historic house. Findings are reported according to these three categories.

Museums responded using data for fiscal year 1988. The overall response rate was 80 percent. For analysis, the sample was weighted for region, type, and size. A full explanation of the statistical method appears in the *Data Report*.

Funding Sources for the 1989 National Museum Survey

Institute of Museum Services

National Endowment for the Arts

National Endowment for the Humanities

National Science Foundation

Philip Morris Companies Inc.

The Rockefeller Foundation

The Dillon Fund

The Max and Victoria Dreyfus Foundation, Inc.

James G. Hanes Memorial Fund/Foundation

Bureau of National Affairs

Museums Count summarizes selected data from the *Data Report* and from the larger survey database. It begins with a profile of America's museums at the end of the 1980s, then examine collections, public service, facilities and human resources, and finances. It highlights informat of significant interest to policy makers, funding agencies, journalists, and all those who work care about, and visit museums. Those seeking detailed or specific findings are advised to cons the *Data Report.* Those interested in the many ways in which museums count—read on.

Data Stratification

Size
Budget adjusted for type–

AQUARIUM
large: $3 million and over
medium: $1 million to $3 million
small: under $1 million

ARBORETUM/BOTANICALGARDEN
small: under $200,000
medium: $200,000 to $1 million
large: $1 million and over

ART MUSEUM
large: $1 million and over
medium: $200,000 to $1 million
small: under $200,000

CHILDREN'S MUSEUM
large: $1 million and over
medium: $200,000 to $1 million
small: under $200,000

GENERAL MUSEUM
large: $1 million and over
medium: $350,000 to $1 million
small: under $350,000

HISTORIC SITE
large: $1 million and over
medium: $350,000 to $1 million
small: under $350,000

HISTORY MUSEUM
large: $1 million and over
medium: $350,000 to $1 million
small: under $350,000

NATURAL HISTORY/ANTHROPOLOGY MUSEUM
large: $1 million and over
medium: $250,000 to $1 million
small: under $250,000

NATURE CENTER
large: $800,000 and over
medium: $250,000 to $800,000
small: under $250,000

PLANETARIUM
large: $1 million and over
medium: $250,000 to $1 million
small: under $250,000

**SCIENCE MUSEUM/
TECHNOLOGY CENTER**
large: $5 million and over
medium: $1 million to $5 million
small: under $1 million

SPECIALIZED MUSEUM
large: $1 million and over
medium: $350,000 to $1 million
small: under $350,000

ZOO
large: $3 million and over
medium: $1 million to $3 million
small: under $1 million

2

HIGHLIGHTS OF FINDINGS

General Profile

There are 8,200 museums in the United States, with more than 15,000 sites:

    55 percent are historic sites or history museums

    15 percent are art museums

    15 percent are science-related museums.

There is one museum or museum site for every 16,000 Americans.

Museums are distributed throughout the United States in roughly the same proportion as the population.

Museum budgets total $4 billion:

    38 percent have annual budgets of $50,000 or less

    57 percent have annual budgets of $100,000 or less

    8 percent have annual budgets of $1,000,000 or more.

When museum type and budget size are considered, 81 percent of museums can be classified as small, 12 percent as medium, and 7 percent as large.

75 percent of museums were founded since 1950.

59 percent of museums are governed as or by private nonprofit organizations; 41 percent are run by government.

70 percent of museums are operated as a subsidiary of an overseeing organization.

Collections

93 percent of museums have permanent collections.

The permanent collections of museums include three-quarters of a billion individual objects or specimens and small objects counted in lots:

    50 percent are natural materials

    25 percent are anthropological and archaeological materials

    12 percent are art objects

    10 percent are history materials.

Of the objects, specimens, and lots held in museum collections:

    58 percent are held by natural history and anthropology museums

Left: African Shrine Gallery, Seattle Art Museum.

Photo by Susan Dirk.

23 percent are held by history museums and historic sites

2 percent are held by art museums.

16 percent of museums have a specific cultural or ethnic focus in their collections.

Public Service

60 percent of museums are open to the public 52 weeks of the year.

24 percent of museums are open to the public 50 hours a week or more.

Museums attract more than a half-billion visits a year—the equivalent of 2 visits per American per year.

From 1986 to 1988, museum visits increased by 10 percent.

Museums and museum programs, including off-site programs, attract 678 million participants annually.

On average, every American visits a museum or participates in a museum program three times year.

On average, every school child in America visits a museum in a school group or participates in one museum program a year.

Museums produced 49,000 exhibitions in 1988, an increase of 23 percent over 1986.

Facilities and Human Resources

Museums are responsible for 222 million square feet of interior space—the equivalent of nearly Pentagons or 100 Empire State Buildings.

The federal government owns and maintains 76 percent of the exterior acreage owned by all museums.

59 percent of museums undertook a major renovation in the last 10 years.

15 percent of museums moved to a new building in the last 10 years.

The total amount of museum square footage increased by more than 15 percent in the last 10 years.

Museums employ 92,000 people full time and 56,000 people part time.

Museums have 35,000 full-time volunteers and 342,000 part-time volunteers.

For every paid staff member, 2.5 people volunteer their time and services to museums.

Of Americans age 18 and older, one in 480 is a museum volunteer.

Finances

Museum budgets total $4 billion annually, close to the budget of the state of Oregon and about five times the annual administrative budget of the United Nations.

Of total museum income:

   two-fifths is from government sources

   two-fifths is from investments and other sources of earned income

   one-fifth is from private contributions.

Of total government allocations to museums in 1988:

   41 percent was from the federal government

   20 percent was from state governments

   34 percent was from local governments

   5 percent was from other government sources.

One-half of museums have endowment funds.

The total value of museum endowments is $14 billion. Of this total:

   93 percent is held by large museums

   76 percent is held by art museums

   96 percent is held by privately run museums.

   55 percent of museums charge admission.

The median admission fee for a nonmember adult is $2 and for a nonmember child, $1.

American museums have 9 million members.

One American in 28 is a museum member.

The median membership fee for individuals is $15 and for families, $25.

54 percent of museum operating expenses go for personnel.

3

GENERAL PROFILE

THERE ARE 8,200 MUSEUMS IN THE UNITED STATES and its territories, one for every 30,000 people reported in the 1988 census estimate. Many museums operate several branches, and if each site is counted individually, the country has more than 15,600 museums. That's one for every 16,000 Americans.

It makes sense to correlate museums with people, because museums reflect public interests. Museums are established by dedicated individuals and sustained through their service to community and nation. As communities grow, their citizens build museums. Across the country, museums can be found in even the smallest towns, and independent communities of 50,000 or more almost invariably have at least one museum. Indeed, museums are hallmarks of American civilization and civic life.

Region
Museums are distributed throughout the United States in roughly the same proportion as the population. For example, the New England region, with 5 percent of the U.S. population, has 7 percent of U.S. museums, while the Western region, with 18 percent of the population, has 16 percent of the museums. The greatest disparity is seen in the Mountain/Plains region, where 13 percent of the population sustains 17 percent of the nation's museums.

Type
More than half of American museums are history museums and historic sites. As historic sites constitute one-quarter of American museums, and nearly one-half of all history museums operate at least one additional branch (likely a historic site), the historic house museum or historic site is the single most common type of museum in America. This preponderance testifies to Americans' well-known interest in their history, both national and local. Nearly one-quarter of the nation's history museums and historic sites are located in the Southeastern region, reflecting the American South's strong ties to its past.

Fifteen percent of America's museums are art museums, and another 15 percent are science related, including aquariums, arboretums and botanical gardens, natural history and anthropology museums, nature centers, planetariums, science centers, and zoos. More than half of natural history and anthropology museums operate at least one additional branch, and more than one-quarter of all natural history and anthropology museums are in the West, again confirming the tendency of museums to represent regional resources and interests.

Other types of museums defined in the 1989 National Museum Survey include children's or youth museums, general museums (those for which two or more disciplines are equally applicable), and specialized museums (those with a single distinct subject or for which no other category is appropriate).

Left: Philadelphia Museum of Art.

Number of Museums by Type and Budget Size

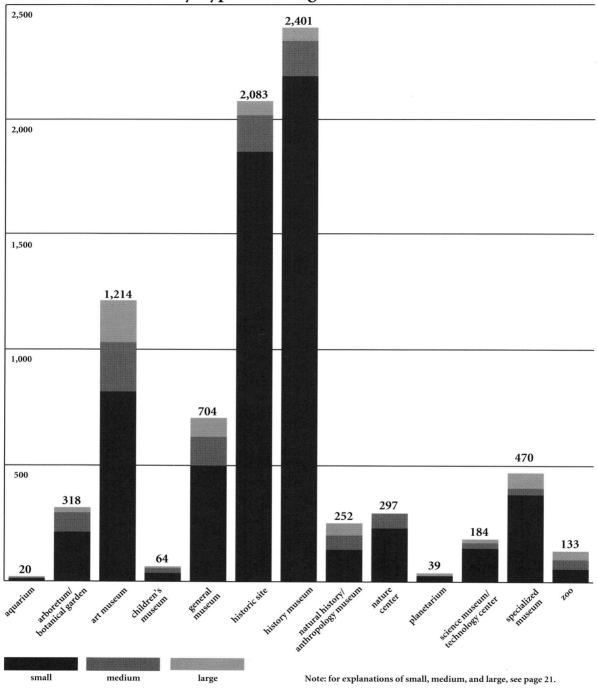

small   medium   large

Note: for explanations of small, medium, and large, see page 21.

Number of Museums by Budget Size and Region

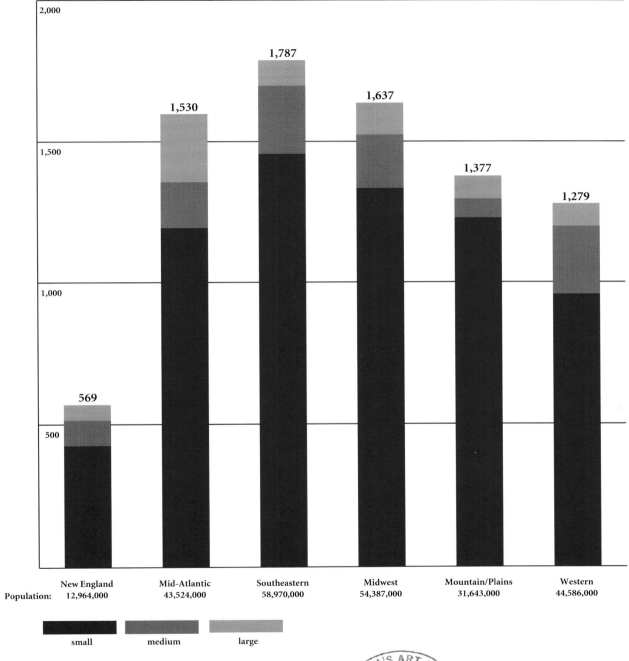

New England	Mid-Atlantic	Southeastern
Population: 12,964,000	43,524,000	58,970,000

Midwest	Mountain/Plains	Western
54,387,000	31,643,000	44,586,000

small   medium   large

DEACCESSIONED

Distribution of Museums by Type

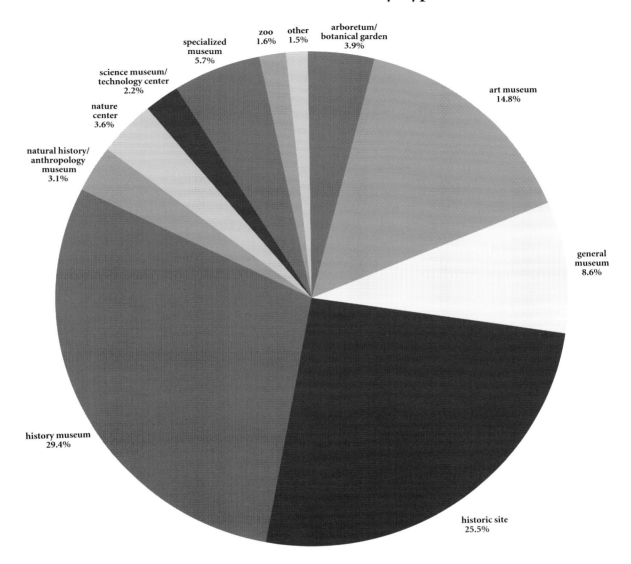

zoo
1.6%

other
1.5%

arboretum/
botanical garden
3.9%

specialized
museum
5.7%

science museum/
technology center
2.2%

nature
center
3.6%

natural history/
anthropology
museum
3.1%

art museum
14.8%

general
museum
8.6%

history museum
29.4%

historic site
25.5%

Note: "other" includes aquarium 0.2%, children's museum 0.8%, and planetarium 0.5%.

Number of Museums and Secondary Sites

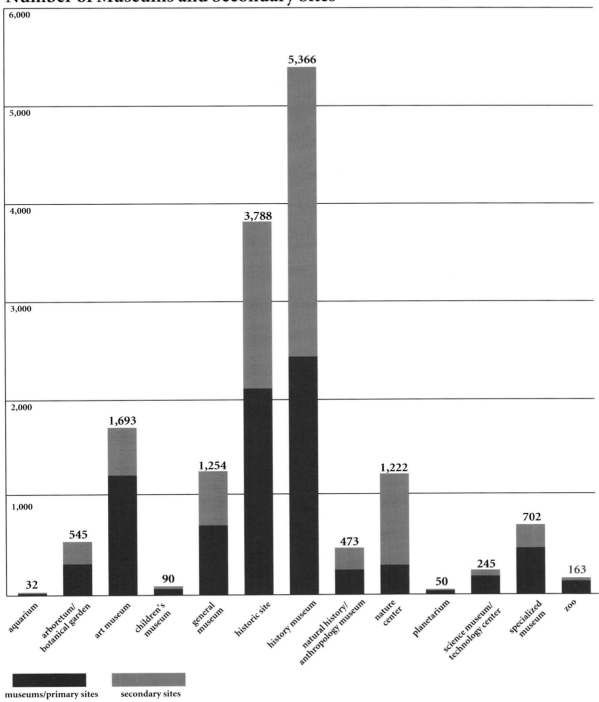

museums/primary sites   secondary sites

Distribution of Museums by Budget Size

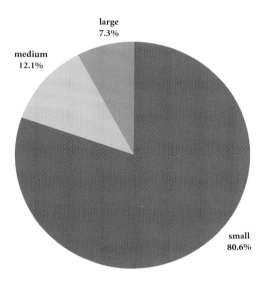

large
7.3%

medium
12.1%

small
80.6%

Size

Using budget size as an indicator, museums in the United States are generally small institutions. More than half of them have annual incomes of less than $100,000, and, of these, two-thirds have incomes of $50,000 or less. When budget size is adjusted for museum type, four out of five American museums can be categorized as small. Only 8 percent of American museums have annual budgets of more than $1 million. These museums are categorized as large; more of them are in the Mid-Atlantic region than in any other. More small museums are in the Southeastern region. Art museums have the largest aggregate budgets of museum types.

Age

The most significant fact about the age of America's museums is their relative youth. Only 4 percent were founded before 1900. Three-quarters have been founded since 1950 and 40 percent since 1970, testifying to a great surge of public interest in museums and to a rapidly expanding corps of museum professionals and specialists. The 1970s witnessed the largest increase ever in the number of museums: three out of 10 were founded in that Bicentennial decade. As people build communities, they build museums: most of the nation's oldest museums are along the East Coast, and many of the younger ones are in the West.

Among the museum types categorized here, zoos are the oldest. Half of America's zoos were founded before 1940. Natural history museums are also a well-established type, with about one in three more than a half century old. While all types of museums have grown at a comparable rate over the past decade, the newest museum type is the children's museum, more than three-quarters of which have been founded in the past 25 years. Nature centers and science centers are also relatively new, with more than half established since 1970. In recent years, the number of museums founded as noncollecting institutions has grown, with the median date of establishment for these institutions being 1975.

The shift in distribution of types—from zoos and natural history and anthropology museums to children's museums, nature centers, and science centers—testifies to the responsiveness of the museum as an institution to trends in scholarship and public demand for education.

Governance

Museums in the United States are grass-roots organizations. Most were founded by intensely dedicated individuals acting in a private capacity for public benefit. As democratic institutions organized to meet local needs, their forms of governance vary widely and are difficult to categorize. Each museum has, however, a governing authority—an entity that has legal and fiduciary responsibility for the museum. The governing authority may or may not own the collection and the physical facility. A museum's building and grounds, for example, may be city property, while its collection and programs are the responsibility of a separate board of directors. A museum's governing authority may be a not-for-profit board, an appointed commission, a governmental body, or a board of university regents. Members of governing authorities generally serve as trustees, without financial compensation.

Total Operating Income by Museum Type

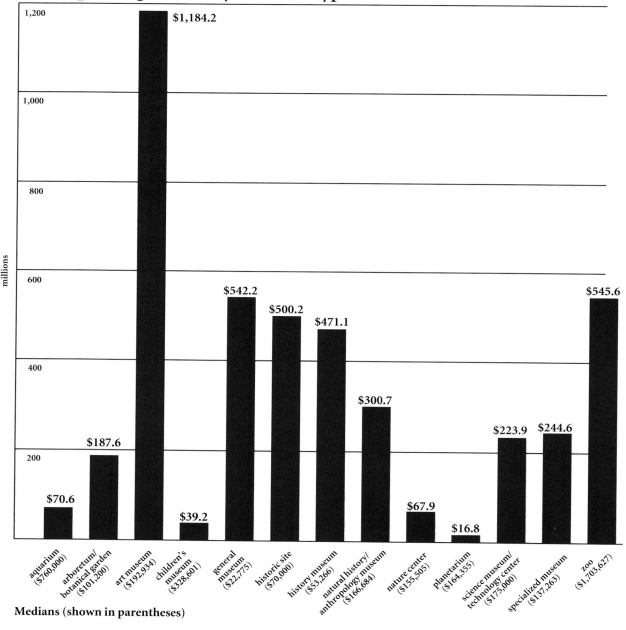

1,200	$1,184.2
1,000	
800	
600	$542.2 $500.2 $471.1 $545.6
400	$300.7
200	$187.6 $223.9 $244.6
	$70.6 $39.2 $67.9 $16.8

millions

Medians (shown in parentheses)

aquarium ($760,000)
arboretum/ botanical garden ($101,200)
art museum ($192,934)
children's museum ($328,601)
general museum ($22,775)
historic site ($70,000)
history museum ($3,266)
natural history/ anthropology museum ($166,684)
nature center ($155,505)
Planetarium ($164,355)
science museum/ technology center ($175,000)
specialized museum ($137,263)
zoo ($1,703,627)

Number of Museums Established by Decade, 1900-1980

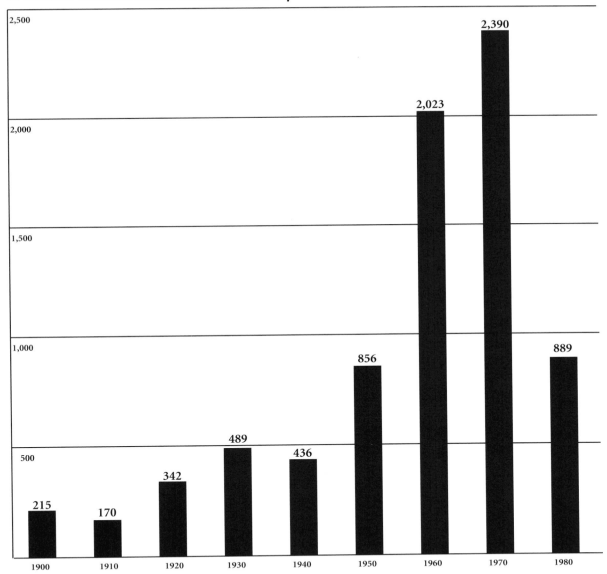

Note: number of museums established before 1900: 365.

Distribution of Museums
by Governing Authority, 1979

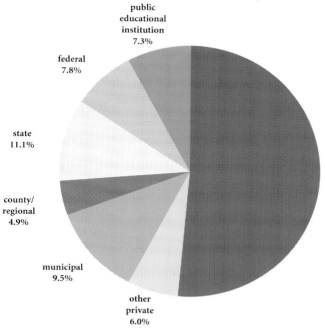

public
educational
institution
7.3%

federal
7.8%

state
11.1%

county/
regional
4.9%

municipal
9.5%

other
private
6.0%

private
nonprofit
53.4%

Note: government-run museums represent 40.6% of the total, and privately run museums, 59.4%.

Distribution of Museums
by Governing Authority, 1988

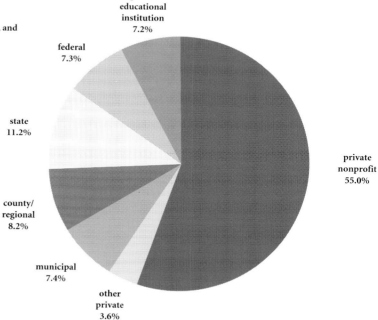

public
educational
institution
7.2%

federal
7.3%

state
11.2%

county/
regional
8.2%

municipal
7.4%

other
private
3.6%

private
nonprofit
55.0%

Note: government-run museums represent 41.3% of the total, and privately run museums, 58.6%.

Perhaps the most distinct division in museum governance is between those institutions that are privately run (59 percent) and those that are run by government (41 percent). Privately run museums are those governed as or by private nonprofit organizations or associations, including private schools or colleges and churches or denominational groups. These museums are private in terms of governing organization only; all of them are open to and serve the public. Their sources of support may be either private or public or, most likely, a combination of both. Government-run museums are governed by an agency at the municipal, county, regional, state, or federal level, or by a public college or school district. For the past decade, the three-fifths/two-fifths split between privately run museums and government-run museums has remained constant.

The private nonprofit organization is the most common form of America's museums, constituting 55 percent of all museums and 94 percent of privately run museums. Other privately run museums, operated by private schools and colleges, religious organizations, or other entities, constitute less than 4 percent of America's museums.

Among government-run museums, nearly half are operated by states and municipalities. Together, state and city museums constitute about one-fifth of the nation's museums. Only 7 percent of America's museums are operated by the federal government, compared to 80 percent in France and 5 percent in England. While the total number of government-run museums has remained fairly constant in the past 10 years, there have been some small shifts within that category. For example, the number of county and regional museums has increased from 5 to 8 percent of the total number of museums. This category includes museums whose governing authorities are special tax districts, and its growth probably reflects a general trend in local government toward regional authority. The percentage of museums run by private colleges or universities has decreased, from more than 3 percent to less than 2 percent, while the percentage of museums run by public colleges or universities has remained steady at about 6 percent.

For the majority of museums, both facilities and collections are owned and operated by the governing authority. But 27 percent of museums have facilities owned or operated separately, and 11 percent have collections owned and operated separately.

Number of Museums by Region and Governing Authority

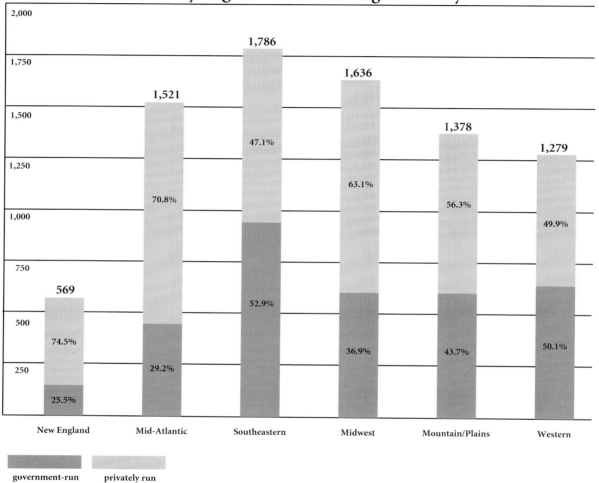

| | government-run | privately run |

Nearly 70 percent of America's museums are operated as an agency of a larger organization, called a parent in the 1989 National Museum Survey. An example might be a historic site operated by a historical society or a nature center run by a regional park system. Certain types of museums are more likely than others to be operated as part of a larger organization. Of planetariums, for example, 93 percent are operated by a parent, while at the other end of the spectrum, only 23 percent of children's museums are operated this way.

Two-thirds of all museums—both privately run and government-run, both those operated by parent organizations and those not—are governed by a board with fiduciary responsibility. Some museums not reporting boards are run by parent organizations with boards responsible for the museum and other agencies. One-third of all museum boards have 10 or fewer members, but a few have more than 60. Nearly 38 percent of museum boards have 11–20 members. Just over half the boards limit the continuous service of members. The nearly 70,000 individuals in the United States who, as volunteers, accept governance responsibilities for museums are testimony to the compelling public purposes these institutions serve.

Profiles by Type

The following profiles present a generalized picture of museums, their varied sizes, structures, activities, services, and resources.[1]

All Museums

Number of museums: 8,179
Number of sites: 15,623

Distribution by size:
   Large: 7%
   Medium: 12%
   Small: 81%
Regional distribution:
   New England: 7%
   Mid-Atlantic: 19%
   Southeastern: 22%
   Midwest: 20%
   Mountain/Plains: 17%
   Western: 16%
Date of establishment: 55% established since 1965
Distribution by governing authority:
   Privately run: 59%
   Government-run: 41%
Percent with a permanent collection: 93%
Attendance:
   Total: 565,843,000
   Median: 50,000
Schoolchildren in groups served:
   Total: 48,827,000
   Median: 16,700

Exhibitions produced:
   Total: 49,000
   Median: 5
Interior square footage:
   Total: 221,713,000
   Median: 8,000
Exterior Acreage:
   Total: 22,667,000
   Median: 8
Staff:
   Paid:
      Total full time: 92,000
      Median full time: 7
      Total part time: 56,000
      Median part time: 5
   Volunteer:
      Total full time: 35,000
      Total part time: 342,000
Budget:
   Total operating income: $4,394,740,000
   Median operating income: $86,656
Endowment:
   Total value: $13,909,842,000
   Median endowment: $125,000
   Percent with endowment: 50%
Median admission fees (for nonmember adult
   Fixed: $2.00
   Suggested: $2.00

Aquariums

Number of museums: 20
Number of sites: 32

Distribution by size:
  Large ($3 million and over): 26%
  Medium ($1 million to $3 million): 20%
  Small (under $1 million): 54%
Regional distribution:
  New England: 16%
  Mid-Atlantic: 11%
  Southeastern: 30%
  Midwest: 7%
  Mountain/Plains: 15%
  Western: 21%
Date of establishment: 57% established since 1975
Distribution by governing authority:
  Privately run: 30%
  Government-run: 70%
Percent with a permanent collection: 80%
Attendance:
  Total: 13,535,000
  Median: 560,375
Schoolchildren in groups served:
  Total: 1,211,000
  Median: 24,585

Exhibitions produced:
  Total: 51
  Median: 3
Interior square footage:
  Total: 1,341,000
  Median: 41,000
Exterior Acreage:
  Total: 780
  Median: 4
Staff:
  Paid:
      Total full time: 1,100
      Median full time: 24.5
      Total part time: 420
      Median part time: 6
  Volunteer:
      Total full time: 780
      Total part time: 1,300
Budget:
  Total operating income: $70,552,000
  Median operating income: $760,000
Endowment:
  Total value: $22,901,000
  Median endowment: $7,200,000
  Percent with endowment: 44%
Median admission fees (for nonmember adult):
  Fixed: $3.75
  Suggested: none

Arboretums and Botanical Gardens

Number of museums: 318
Number of sites: 545

Distribution by size:
  Large ($1 million and over): 7%
  Medium ($200,000 to $1 million): 27%
  Small (under $200,000): 66%
Regional distribution:
  New England: 2%
  Mid-Atlantic: 23%
  Southeastern: 24%
  Midwest: 36%
  Mountain/Plains: 5%
  Western: 11%
Date of establishment: 53% established since
  1965
Distribution by governing authority:
  Privately run: 44%
  Government-run: 56%
Percent with a permanent collection: 87%
Attendance:
  Total: 26,101,000
  Median: 70,000
Schoolchildren in groups served:
  Total: 658,000
  Median: 5,000

Exhibitions produced:
  Total: 1,000
  Median: 2
Interior square footage:
  Total: 4,262,000
  Median: 5,183
Exterior acreage:
  Total: 91,000
  Median: 40
Staff:
  Paid:
       Total full time: 8,100
       Median full time: 16
       Total part time: 2,200
       Median part time: 5
  Volunteer:
       Total full time: 920
       Total part time: 11,000
Budget:
  Total operating income: $187,567,000
  Median operating income: $101,200
Endowment:
  Total value: $636,493,000
  Median endowment: $500,000
  Percent with endowment: 56%
Median admission fees (for nonmember adul
  Fixed: $4.00
  Suggested: none

Art Museums

Number of museums: 1,214
Number of sites: 1,693

Distribution by size:
   Large ($1 million and over): 15%
   Medium ($200,000 to $1 million): 18%
   Small (under $200,000): 67%
Regional distribution:
   New England: 10%
   Mid-Atlantic: 23%
   Southeastern: 18%
   Midwest: 15%
   Mountain/Plains: 13%
   Western: 21%
Date of establishment: 50% established since
   1970
Distribution by governing authority:
   Privately run: 69%
   Government-run: 31%
Percent with a permanent collection: 82%
Attendance:
   Total: 75,920,000
   Median: 60,000
Schoolchildren in groups served:
   Total: 5,158,000
   Median: 14,500

Exhibitions produced:
   Total: 14,000
   Median: 9
Interior square footage:
   Total: 33,041,000
   Median: 8,000
Exterior acreage:
   Total: 39,000
   Median: 5
Staff:
   Paid:
         Total full time: 20,000
         Median full time: 15
         Total part time: 11,00
         Median part time: 8.5
   Volunteer:
         Total full time: 3,400
         Total part time: 53,000
Budget:
   Total operating income: $1,184,182,000
   Median operating income: $192,934
Endowment:
   Total value: $10,541,334,000
   Median endowment: $577,054
   Percent with endowment: 54%
Median admission fees (for nonmember adult):
   Fixed: $3.00
   Suggested: $3.00

Children's Museums

Number of museums: 64
Number of sites: 90

Distribution by size:
    Large ($1 million and over): 11%
    Medium ($200,000 to $1 million): 32%
    Small (under $200,000): 57%
Regional distribution:
    New England: 14%
    Mid-Atlantic: 19%
    Southeastern: 24%
    Midwest: 17%
    Mountain/Plains: 7%
    Western: 19%
Date of establishment: 68% established since
    1975
Distribution by governing authority:
    Privately run: 89%
    Government-run: 11%
Percent with a permanent collection: 68%
Attendance:
    Total: 7,365,000
    Median: 64,000
Schoolchildren in groups served:
    Total: 1,083,000
    Median: 21,734

Exhibitions produced:
    Total: 430
    Median: 5
Interior square footage:
    Total: 1,274,000
    Median: 10,000
Exterior acreage:
    Total: 80
    Median: 2
Staff:
    Paid:
        Total full time: 800
        Median full time: 6
        Total part time: 800
        Median part time: 7
    Volunteer:
        Total full time: 470
        Total part time: 2,400
Budget:
    Total operating income: $39,249,000
    Median operating income: $328,601
Endowment:
    Total value: $91,457,000
    Median endowment: $90,000
    Percent with endowment: 61%
Median admission fees (for nonmember adu
    Fixed: $2.50
    Suggested: $2.00

General Museums

Number of museums: 704
Number of sites: 1,254

Distribution by size:
   Large ($1 million and over): 11%
   Medium ($350,000 to $1 million): 18%
   Small (under $350,000): 71%
Regional distribution:
   New England: 9%
   Mid-Atlantic: 17%
   Southeastern: 8%
   Midwest: 31%
   Mountain/Plains: 25%
   Western: 11%
Date of establishment: 52% established since
   1960
Distribution by governing authority:
   Privately run: 67%
   Government-run: 33%
Percent with a permanent collection: 99%
Attendance:
   Total: 32,087,000
   Median: 53,000
Schoolchildren in groups served:
   Total: 4,297,000
   Median: 9,629

Exhibitions produced:
   Total: 5,400
   Median: 9
Interior square footage:
   Total: 15,643,000
   Median: 10,000
Exterior acreage:
   Total: 3,403,000
   Median: 4
Staff:
   Paid:
      Total full time: 5,300
      Median full time: 9.5
      Total part time: 3,700
      Median part time: 6
   Volunteer:
      Total full time: 2,400
      Total part time: 29,000
Budget:
   Total operating income: $542,180,000
   Median operating income: $22,775[2]
Endowment:
   Total value: $531,793,000
   Median endowment: $105,485
   Percent with endowment: 57%
Median admission fees (for nonmember adult):
   Fixed: $1.50
   Suggested: $2.00

Historic Sites

Number of museums: 2,083
Number of sites: 3,788

Distribution by size:
    Large ($1 million and over): 3%
    Medium ($350,000 to $1 million): 8%
    Small (under $350,000): 89%
Regional distribution:
    New England: 8%
    Mid-Atlantic: 20%
    Southeastern: 29%
    Midwest: 13%
    Mountain/Plains: 18%
    Western: 12%
Date of establishment: 60% established since
    1960
Distribution by governing authority:
    Privately run: 48%
    Government-run: 52%
Percent with a permanent collection: 99%
Attendance:
    Total: 111,027,000
    Median: 32,187
Schoolchildren in groups served:
    Total: 8,010,000
    Median: 5,061

Exhibitions produced:
    Total: 5,100
    Median: 3
Interior square footage:
    Total: 37,365,000
    Median: 7,000
Exterior acreage:
    Total: 1,331,000
    Median: 12
Staff:
    Paid:
        Total full time: 15,000
        Median full time: 4
        Total part time: 11,000
        Median part time: 3
    Volunteer:
        Total full time: 5,700
        Total part time: 114,000
Budget:
    Total operating income: $500,242,000
    Median operating income: $70,000
Endowment:
    Total value: $457,503,000
    Median endowment: $113,332
    Percent with endowment: 35%
Median admission fees (for nonmember adu
    Fixed: $2.00
    Suggested: $1.00

History Museums

Number of museums: 2,401
Number of sites: 5,366

Distribution by size:
Large ($1 million and over): 2%
Medium ($350,000 to $1 million): 6%
Small (under $350,000): 91%
Regional distribution:
New England: 6%
Mid-Atlantic: 13%
Southeastern: 18%
Midwest: 24%
Mountain/Plains: 20%
Western: 19%
Date of establishment: 56% established since
1965
Distribution by governing authority:
Privately run: 66%
Government-run: 34%
Percent with a permanent collection: 98%
Attendance:
Total: 71,807,000
Median: 21,857
Schoolchildren in groups served:
Total: 7,061,000
Median: 16,220

Exhibitions produced:
Total: 17,000
Median: 5
Interior square footage:
Total: 42,348,000
Median: 7,500
Exterior acreage:
Total: 4,950,000
Median: 3
Staff:
Paid:
Total full time: 12,300
Median full time: 3
Total part time: 8,700
Median part time: 3
Volunteer:
Total full time: 13,000
Total part time: 56,000
Budget:
Total operating income: $471,150,000
Median operating income: $53,266
Endowment:
Total value: $654,530,000
Median endowment: $110,000
Percent with endowment: 61%
Median admission fees (for nonmember adult):
Fixed: $2.00
Suggested: $2.00

Natural History and Anthropology Museums

Number of museums: 252
Number of sites: 473

Distribution by size:
  Large ($1 million and over): 21%
  Medium ($250,000 to $1 million): 25%
  Small (under $250,000): 55%
Regional distribution:
  New England: 8%
  Mid-Atlantic: 19%
  Southeastern: 17%
  Midwest: 15%
  Mountain/Plains: 13%
  Western: 28%
Date of establishment: 55% established since
  1960
Distribution by governing authority:
  Privately run: 38%
  Government-run: 62%
Percent with a permanent collection: 93%
Attendance:
  Total: 50,795,000
  Median: 56,470
Schoolchildren in groups served:
  Total: 4,094,000
  Median: 16,270

Exhibitions produced:
  Total: 1,300
  Median: 4
Interior square footage:
  Total: 11,384,000
  Median: 11,000
Exterior acreage:
  Total: 10,161,000
  Median: 67
Staff:
  Paid:
      Total full time: 6,300
      Median full time: 10
      Total part time: 2,80
      Median part time: 8
  Volunteer:
      Total full time: 1,300
      Total part time: 11,000
Budget:
  Total operating income: $300,737,000
  Median operating income: $166,684
Endowment:
  Total value: $461,268,000
  Median endowment: $1,118,611
  Percent with endowment: 45%
Median admission fees (for nonmember adu
  Fixed: $2.00
  Suggested: $3.00

Nature Centers

Number of museums: 297
Number of sites: 1,222

Distribution by size:
  Large ($800,000 and over): 1%
  Medium ($250,000 to $800,000): 22%
  Small (under $250,000): 77%
Regional distribution:
  New England: 9%
  Mid-Atlantic: 19%
  Southeastern: 27%
  Midwest: 27%
  Mountain/Plains: 11%
  Western: 7%
Date of establishment: 57% established since
  1970
Distribution by governing authority:
  Privately run: 38%
  Government-run: 62%
Percent with a permanent collection: 76%
Attendance:
  Total: 21,840,000
  Median: 29,199
Schoolchildren in groups served:
  Total: 2,809,000
  Median: 8,000

Exhibitions produced:
  Total: 910
  Median: 4
Interior square footage:
  Total: 1,626,000
  Median: 3,700
Exterior acreage:
  Total: 2,592,000
  Median: 212
Staff:
  Paid:
      Total full time: 2,000
      Median full time: 5
      Total part time: 1,600
      Median part time: 3
  Volunteer:
      Total full time: 680
      Total part time: 14,000
Budget:
  Total operating income: $67,928,000
  Median operating income: $155,505
Endowment:
  Total value: $79,947,000
  Median endowment: $350,000
  Percent with endowment: 46%
Median admission fees (for nonmember adult):
  Fixed: $2.00
  Suggested: none

Planetariums

Number of museums: 39
Number of sites: 50

Distribution by size:
  Large ($1 million and over): 3%
  Medium ($250,000 to $1 million): 30%
  Small (under $250,000): 67%
Regional distribution:
  New England: 7%
  Mid-Atlantic: 6%
  Southeastern: 41%
  Midwest: 32%
  Mountain/Plains: 0%[3]
  Western: 15%
Date of establishment: 54% established since
  1965
Distribution by governing authority:
  Privately run: 9%
  Government-run: 91%
Percent with a permanent collection: 87%
Attendance:
  Total: 6,112,000
  Median: 35,500
Schoolchildren in groups served:
  Total: 887,000
  Median: 20,000

Exhibitions produced:
  Total: 160
  Median: 5
Interior square footage:
  Total: 441,000
  Median: 6,100
Exterior acreage:
  Total: 27
  Median: 2
Staff:
  Paid:
      Total full time: 240
      Median full time: 3.5
      Total part time: 330
      Median part time: 5
  Volunteer:
      Total full time: 7
      Total part time: 300
Budget:
  Total operating income: $16,827,000
  Median operating income: $164,355
Endowment:
  Total value: $18,236,000
  Median endowment: $5,000,000
  Percent with endowment: 36%
Median admission fees (for nonmember adult
  Fixed: $3.00
  Suggested: none

Science Museums and Technology Centers

Number of museums: 184
Number of sites: 245

Distribution by size:
   Large ($5 million and over): 9%
   Medium ($1 million to $5 million): 13%
   Small (under $1 million): 78%
Regional distribution:
   New England: 3%
   Mid-Atlantic: 22%
   Southeastern: 30%
   Midwest: 27%
   Mountain/Plains: 11%
   Western: 7%
Date of establishment: 58% established since
   1970
Distribution by governing authority:
   Privately run: 66%
   Government-run: 34%
Percent with a permanent collection: 90%
Attendance:
   Total: 45,574,000
   Median: 94,343
Schoolchildren in groups served:
   Total: 4,088,000
   Median: 14,000

Exhibitions produced:
   Total: 1,260
   Median: 4
Interior square footage:
   Total: 7,475,000
   Median: 10,000
Exterior acreage:
   Total: 72,000
   Median: 20
Staff:
   Paid:
      Total full time: 4,070
      Median full time: 16
      Total part time: 3,900
      Median part time: 9.5
   Volunteer:
      Total full time: 140
      Total part time: 23,000
Budget:
   Total operating income: $223,892,000
   Median operating income: $175,000
Endowment:
   Total value: $138,668,000
   Median endowment: $751,500
   Percent with endowment: 45%
Median admission fees (for nonmember adult):
   Fixed: $3.50
   Suggested: $2.50

Specialized Museums

Number of museums: 470
Number of sites: 702

Distribution by size:
  Large ($1 million and over): 14%
  Medium ($350,000 to $1 million): 6%
  Small (under $350,000): 80%
Regional distribution:
  New England: 1%
  Mid-Atlantic: 31%
  Southeastern: 33%
  Midwest: 13%
  Mountain/Plains: 8%
  Western: 14%
Date of establishment: 53% established since
  1975
Distribution by governing authority:
  Privately run: 71%
  Government-run: 29%
Percent with a permanent collection: 92%
Attendance:
  Total: 22,516,000
  Median: 17,974
Schoolchildren in groups served:
  Total: 3,831,000
  Median: 6,000

Exhibitions produced:
  Total: 1,800
  Median: 4
Interior square footage:
  Total: 11,557,000
  Median: 9,284
Exterior acreage:
  Total: 14,000
  Median: 4
Staff:
  Paid:
      Total full time: 4,500
      Median full time: 4
      Total part time: 2,400
      Median part time: 3
  Volunteer:
      Total full time: 470
      Total part time: 16,000
Budget:
  Total operating income: $244,625,000
  Median operating income: $137,263
Endowment:
  Total value: $255,196,000
  Median endowment: $149,778
  Percent with endowment: 50%
Median admission fees (for nonmember adu
  Fixed: $3.00
  Suggested: $1.00

Zoos

Number of museums: 133
Number of sites: 163

Distribution by size:
    Large ($3 million and over): 28%
    Medium ($1 million to $3 million): 30%
    Small (under $1 million): 42%
Regional distribution:
    New England: 1%
    Mid-Atlantic: 18%
    Southeastern: 18%
    Midwest: 26%
    Mountain/Plains: 25%
    Western: 12%
Date of establishment: 54% established before 1940
Distribution by governing authority:
    Privately run: 33%
    Government-run: 67%
Percent with a permanent collection: 100%
Attendance:
    Total: 81,165,000
    Median: 482,006
Schoolchildren in groups served:
    Total: 5,640,000
    Median: 46,575

Exhibitions produced:
    Total: 200
    Median: 2
Interior square footage:
    Total: 53,955,000
    Median: 75,500
Exterior acreage:
    Total: 14,000
    Median: 48
Staff:
    Paid:
        Total full time: 12,000
        Median full time: 65
        Total part time: 7,400
        Median part time: 14
    Volunteer:
        Total full time: 5,50
        Total part time: 11,000
Budget:
    Total operating income: $545,611,000
    Median operating income: $1,703,627
Endowment:
    Total value: $38,183,000
    Median endowment: $190,000
    Percent with endowment: 37%
Median admission fees (for nonmember adult):
    Fixed: $3.00
    Suggested: none

4

COLLECTIONS

THE MOST TRADITIONAL ACTIVITY OF MUSEUMS IS COLLECTING. As the Commission on Museums for a New Century expressed it, "The act of collecting is more than an institutional expression of a human trait. It is our society's cumulative effort to save ourselves, our history, our natural surroundings, our technological and creative endeavors." In the aggregate, museum collections "represent the whole diversity of the world's cultural, scientific, and natural heritage."

Each museum's collection has its origins in the interests of the museum's founders, and the museum's mission determines how the collection grows. Individual objects may be priceless or common, decorative or utilitarian, human-made or natural, living or nonliving, as large as a historic house or as small as a smear on a slide. They can be quantified and categorized, but numbers in lists cannot convey the values and meanings they hold for individuals, communities, and the nation. Museum collections are America's natural and cultural common wealth.

Museums with and without Collections

Most museums in the United States—93 percent—are traditional collecting institutions. But in recent decades the idea of a museum has expanded to encompass noncollecting institutions, too. Nature centers, science and technology centers, and children's museums often borrow exhibition materials or fabricate objects for educational exhibits and programs. Some of the objects they display and use in educational activities are expendable. Only three-quarters of nature centers and two-thirds of children's museums own collections. The one-fifth of art museums that do not own collections are likely to be art centers, which borrow artworks for exhibition rather than building and maintaining permanent collections. Museums without permanent collections are increasing in number.

They can be quantified and categorized, but numbers in lists cannot convey the values and meanings museums hold for individuals, communities, and the nation

Types and Numbers of Collections

American museums care for nearly three-quarters of a billion objects and specimens and 11 million lots—small objects counted in groups, such as a collection of potsherds from a single archeological site. By far the greatest proportion of total museum collections are owned by natural history and anthropology museums, a long-established museum type that originally defined its mission as collecting examples of natural forms and material culture from around the world.

Left: Warm Springs Tribal Museum, Warm Springs, Oregon.
Photograph by John Hughel, Jr.

Museum Collections: Classifications
Used in the 1989 National Museum Survey

Objects/specimens
discrete items: a painting, a mounted bald eagle, a locomotive, 12 yards of historic fabric

Lots/taxa/populations
groups of small objects or specimens counted by the museum as a group rather than individually: potsherds, insects

Archival material
documentary materials excluding printed and bound books: a photograph collection in a historic house, a 19th-century botanist's field notes

Books
printed, bound materials that are in the collection, not simply support it, estimated in square or linear feet: a rare book, an artist's bound journal

Sites/structures
actual count of buildings or sites: a historic farmstead, a house designed by a famous architect

Acres
estimated acres considered part of the permanent collection, excluding land used for recreation and visitor services such as parking lots: a botanical garden, a battlefield

Although constituting only 3 percent of American museums, natural history and anthropolog museums hold 58 percent of the total number of objects, specimens, and lots in American mu um collections. Art museums, although constituting 15 percent of American museums, hold 2 percent. History museums and historic sites, constituting 55 percent of museums, hold 23 per of these collections. The rest of the objects, specimens, and lots in American museum collectio are distributed among other museum types.

Of archival material counted as permanent collections, including scientists' field notes, artis correspondence, and exhibition records (but excluding bound materials that would be reporte books), museums have 4 million cubic feet. This measure translates into more than 3,400 mile material, the distance from Miami to Seattle. General museums, history museums, natural hist and anthropology museums, and specialized museums hold the majority of these materials.

Distribution of Numbers of Objects and Specimens in Permanent Collections by Museum Type

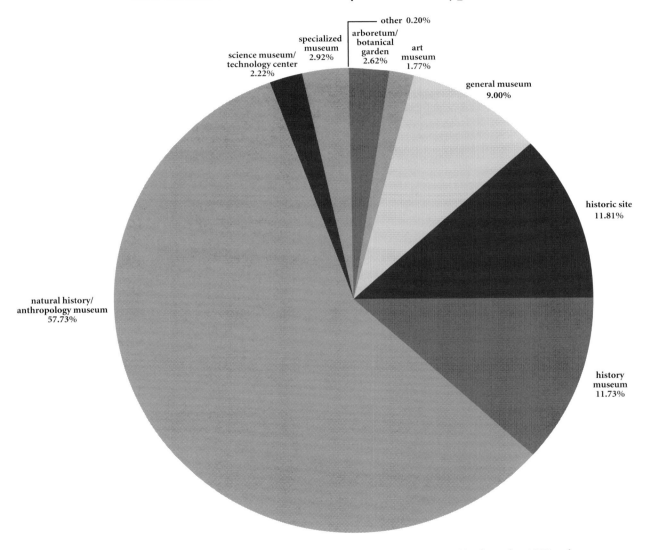

other 0.20%

specialized museum 2.92%

arboretum/ botanical garden 2.62%

science museum/ technology center 2.22%

art museum 1.77%

general museum 9.00%

historic site 11.81%

natural history/ anthropology museum 57.73%

history museum 11.73%

Note: "other" comprises aquarium 0.01%; children's museum 0.05%; nature center 0.02%; planetarium 0.01%; and zoo 0.11%. Lots (small objects and specimens counted in groups) are not included here or in the following chart.

Altogether, museums have more than 7 million volumes of bound materials counted as collections. These are rare books, newspaper clippings, and albums. Again, history museums and natural history and anthropology museums hold the largest proportions of these items.

Some museums count structures and sites as objects in the permanent collections. Museums have 15,000 such sites, most of them—13,500—in the collections of historic sites and history museums.

Finally, some museums count acreage as permanent collections. For botanical gardens and battlefields, this figure might be the entire site; for a historic site, it might include only the area around a historic building. Of the 23 million acres for which museums are responsible, 4 million are held in permanent collections—an area slightly larger than the states of Rhode Island and Connecticut combined. For general museums, the median acreage is two; for historic sites, six; and for natural history and anthropology museums, 77.

Of the total number of objects, specimens, and lots in museums of all types, half are described by these museums as natural collections, which include living and nonliving zoological specimens, living and nonliving botanical specimens, geological specimens, and paleontological specimens. One-quarter are anthropological and archeological materials, including ethnological and ethnographical materials, folk culture artifacts, and physical anthropology specimens. Twelve percent are art collections, including paintings, prints, drawings, graphic arts objects, sculpture, decorative arts objects, costumes, textiles, audiovisual materials, film, photographs (classified as aesthetic rather than historic), and archeological and ethnographic works. Ten percent are historical collections, including structures, furnishings, personal artifacts, tools, equipment, distribution and transportation artifacts, recreation artifacts, and items created as expressions of human thought, such as advertising, art, ceremonial, religious, and documentary artifacts and coins and stamps. The remaining collections were classified in a miscellaneous category called Other.

The mission statements of 16 percent of U.S. museums designate a specific cultural or ethnic focus in collections. Examples are African-American or Jewish museums. Most museums with a cultural or ethnic collecting focus are art museums, historic sites, and natural history and anthropology museums.

Distribution of Objects and Specimens in Permanent Collections by Collection Type

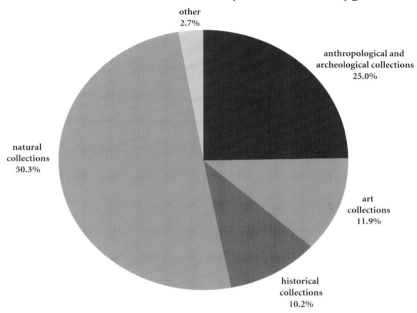

other
2.7%

anthropological and archeological collections
25.0%

art collections
11.9%

historical collections
10.2%

natural collections
50.3%

Collection Records

All told, records have been developed and maintained for about three-fifths of permanent collections in American museums. At least one-tenth of the objects and specimens that have been inventoried have not been catalogued. In general, collection materials grouped in lots are not nearly so well recorded as objects and specimens. The 1989 National Museum Survey confirms that the national need for improving collection records is acute: while about 82 percent of objects and specimens have been inventoried, only 76 percent of these have also been catalogued.

5

PUBLIC SERVICE

MOST MUSEUMS COLLECT AND CARE FOR OBJECTS, but collecting and preserving are not enough to make an institution a museum. To be a museum, an institution does not even have to have a collection. The primary requirement is that it use or exhibit objects to serve the public. Most museums in the United States were founded for avowedly public purposes, often the advancement and diffusion of knowledge.

The public services that museums provide take many forms. Museums sponsor research and make their collections available for study by scholars both inside and outside the museum and the museum community. They loan objects to other institutions for study and exhibition. They use their own and other collections to mount exhibitions that inform and educate. To enhance public understanding and enjoyment, museums provide orientation programs, interpretive demonstrations, tours, classes, workshops, clubs, academic courses, special lectures, films and media programs, library services, live performing arts, and special events like fairs and festivals. They produce radio and television programs, arrange for field trips and travel programs, and organize outreach services. They offer school programs and teacher training. They publish catalogues and books, scientific and scholarly studies, films and videos, television and radio productions, slide and photo sets, curriculum packages, gallery guides, and newsletters. Most museums do some of these things; a few do them all. Of the many kinds of programs offered, tours and special events serve the greatest number of people.

The public services that museums provide take many forms, from research to school programs and teacher training

Hours Open to the Public

Public service begins at the front door. To be considered a museum for the 1989 National Museum Survey, an institution had to be open to the public on a regular basis at least 120 days a year. Three-fifths of museums are open 52 weeks of the year; less than 1 percent are open by special arrangement only. Of museum types, only half of art museums are open all year. Museums not open all year are open an average of 37 weeks annually. Many of these are outdoor or other museums that are seasonal in nature.

Of museums that are open to the public without special arrangement, one-quarter are open more than 50 hours a week and one-third fewer than 30 hours a week. Of museum types, four-fifths of aquariums are open more than 50 hours a week, as are three-quarters of arboretums and botanical gardens. Only 7 percent of art museums and 6 percent of children's museums are open that many hours, perhaps reflecting a common practice among art museums of closing on Mondays and a concentration of hours open by children's museums at times best suited to children. Nearly half of history museums and one-quarter of historic sites are open fewer than 30 hours a week, reflecting their small size, seasonal nature, and heavy reliance on volunteers.

Left: Memphis Zoo.

U.S Population and Total Museum Attendance, 1976–1978 and 1986–1988

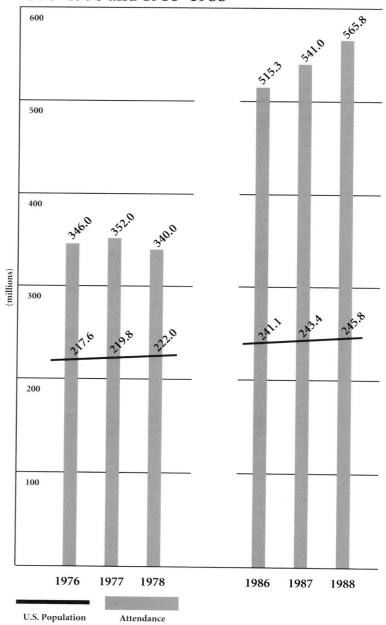

(millions)

600
515.3 · 541.0 · 565.8
500
400
346.0 · 352.0 · 340.0
300
241.1 · 243.4 · 245.8
217.6 · 219.8 · 222.0
200
100

1976 1977 1978   1986 1987 1988

U.S. Population   Attendance

Note: figures for 1976–78 from 1979 Museum Program Survey.

Distribution of Museums by Number of Hours Open per Week

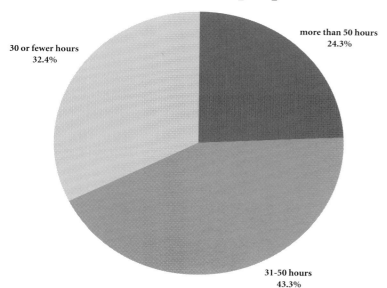

more than 50 hours
24.3%

30 or fewer hours
32.4%

31-50 hours
43.3%

Number of Visits

Museums attract more than half a billion visits a year. That's two visits per person in the United States, though of course museum visiting doesn't work that way: many people visit museums dozens of times each year, while others never visit at all.

Nevertheless, even rough counts suggest that museums are increasing in popularity. The 1979 Museum Program Survey reported nearly 350 million museum visits. Correlated to the 1980 census, that would be about 1.5 visits per person per year. More reliably, the 1989 National Museum Survey tracked museum visits over a three-year period, from 1986 through 1988, and documented that the number of total museum visits increased by 5 percent each year—from 515 million to 541 million to 566 million. Correlated to the 1988 census estimates, that's about 2.3 visits per person per year. Two-thirds of museums arrive at attendance figures through an accurate count; most others estimate the count, but some museums use both methods.

During the period surveyed, all museum types experienced increases in visitation. There were a few fluctuations: for arboretums and botanical gardens, visitation decreased slightly in 1987 but rose again in 1988, while for history museums it fell by 2 percent from 1987 to 1988. Still, the overall trend was up. Visits to general museums increased by the highest rate—by 7 percent in 1987 and again by 13 percent in 1988. Visits to science museums and technology centers increased by 6 percent in 1987 and again by 13 percent in 1988. Aquariums and zoos experienced the highest median attendance in this period: 560,375 and 482,006, respectively. Aquariums and children's museums increased their median attendance by more than 25 percent in 1987 over 1986. The median number of visits to all types of museums in 1988 was 50,000.

Large museums received a disproportionate percentage of the total number of visits. Although constituting 7 percent of museums, they attracted almost half of all museum visits. The median annual attendance at large museums for 1988 was 233,162; for medium-sized museums, 82,000. Government-run museums (41 percent) also received a disproportionately large percentage of the total number of visits: 58 percent. The number of visits to federal museums stands out at more than 20 percent of the total number of museum visits, although they constitute only 7 percent of American museums. This large share is explained in part by the Smithsonian Institution and the large national parks, which attract visitors from across the nation. Predictably, the Mid-Atlantic region, which has both the largest number and highest percentage of the nation's large museums, had a large number of visits—140 million in 1988. But among regions this was only the second highest figure. The museums in the Midwest had a total of 145 million visits.

Distribution of Total Attendance

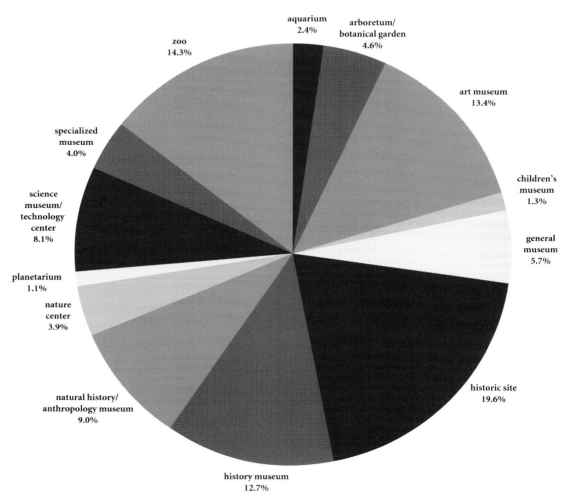

aquarium
2.4%

arboretum/
botanical garden
4.6%

zoo
14.3%

art museum
13.4%

specialized
museum
4.0%

children's
museum
1.3%

science
museum/
technology
center
8.1%

general
museum
5.7%

planetarium
1.1%

nature
center
3.9%

historic site
19.6%

natural history/
anthropology museum
9.0%

history museum
12.7%

Median Attendance

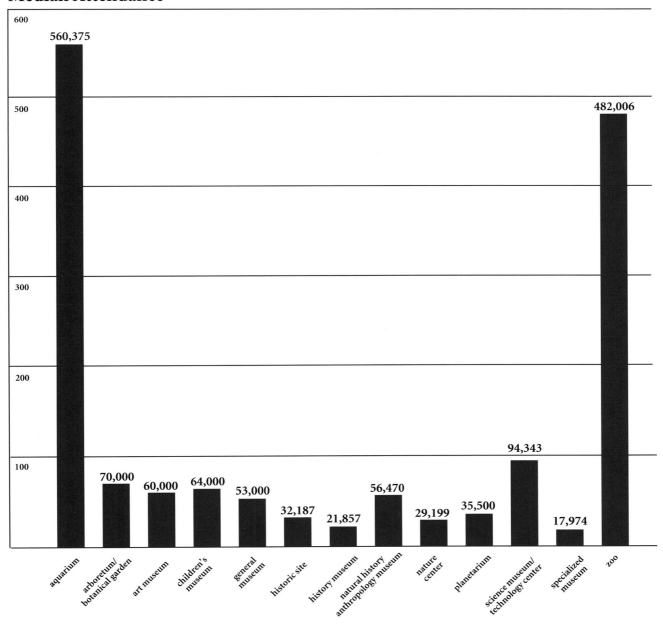

aquarium	560,375
arboretum/botanical garden	70,000
art museum	60,000
children's museum	64,000
general museum	53,000
historic site	32,187
history museum	21,857
natural history anthropology museum	56,470
nature center	29,199
planetarium	35,500
science museum/technology center	94,343
specialized museum	17,974
zoo	482,006

Distribution of Attendance by Governing Authority

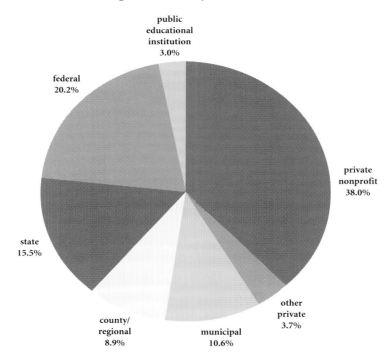

Note: of total attendance, government-run museums reported 58.2%, and privately run museums, 41.7%.

When thinking about museum attendance figures, however, it is important to look at the sm numbers, too. Small museums, two-thirds of which have budgets of less than $50,000, had a median attendance of 15,000 in 1988. They accounted for 30 percent of total museum visitatio that year, indicating that even institutions with very limited financial resources provide signific public service.

Attendance by Budget Size of Museum, 1986–1988

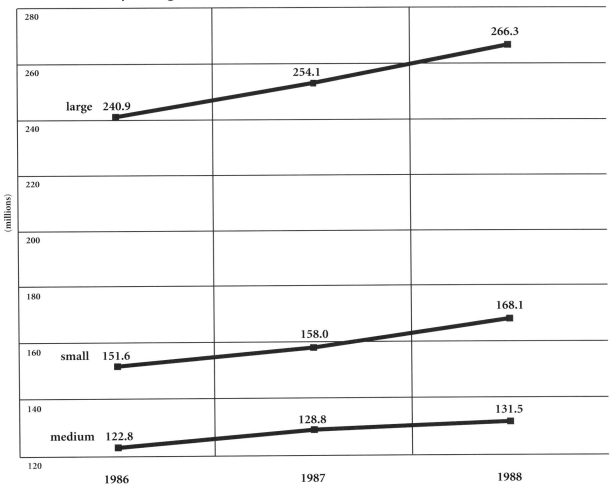

(millions)

	1986	1987	1988
large	240.9	254.1	266.3
small	151.6	158.0	168.1
medium	122.8	128.8	131.5

Attendance and Number of People Served

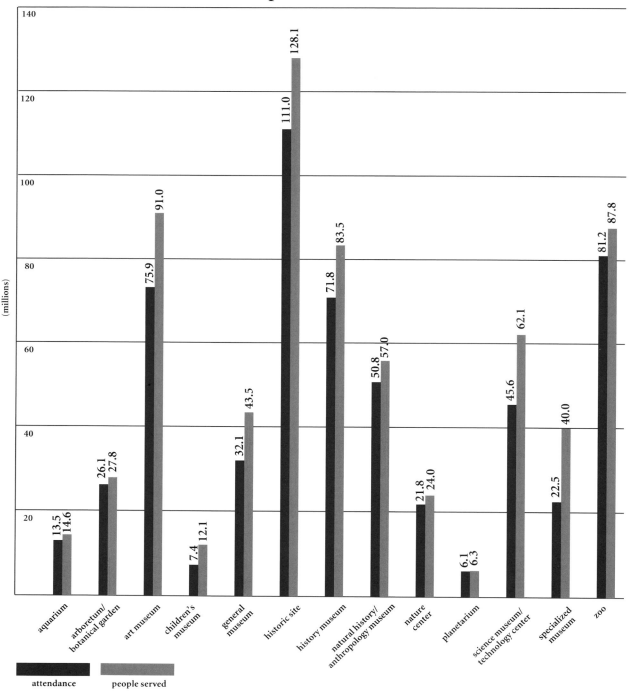

aquarium — attendance 13.5, people served 14.6
arboretum/botanical garden — attendance 26.1, people served 27.8
art museum — attendance 75.9, people served 91.0
children's museum — attendance 7.4, people served 12.1
general museum — attendance 32.1, people served 43.5
historic site — attendance 111.0, people served 128.1
history museum — attendance 71.8, people served 83.5
natural history/anthropology museum — attendance 50.8, people served 57.0
nature center — attendance 21.8, people served 24.0
planetarium — attendance 6.1, people served 6.3
science museum/technology center — attendance 45.6, people served 62.1
specialized museum — attendance 22.5, people served 40.0
zoo — attendance 81.2, people served 87.8

(millions)

■ attendance   ▨ people served

Number of Individuals Served, Including Teachers and Schoolchildren

Each year, museums and museum programs, including off-site programs such as travel and tours, outreach activities, classroom presentations, and academic courses, attract 678 million participants. This figure suggests that, on average, every American visited a museum or participated in a museum program three times in 1988.

Historic sites serve the largest number of individuals—128 million in 1988, or 19 percent of the total. Together historic sites and history museums served 212 million individuals. Zoos, constituting only 2 percent of museums, served 13 percent of the total number of individuals served.

Although constituting 7 percent of the total number of museums, large museums served 45 percent of individuals served in 1988. Government-run museums (41 percent of all museums) served 56 percent. Of government-run museums, federal museums served the largest number—134 million individuals in 1988, or 20 percent of the total served—while constituting only 7 percent of American museums.

America's museums are important educational resources. Forty-nine million of the individuals served by museums in 1988 were children in school groups, a figure that comes uncannily close to the 49.1 million children ages 5–18 estimated by the Census Bureau for that year. While some schoolchildren no doubt went on several field trips to museums during the school year, and some did not go at all, the figures suggest that a great many schoolchildren regularly benefit from class activities built around the educational resources of museums.

Historic sites served the largest number of schoolchildren—8 million. Together, historic sites and history museums served 15 million schoolchildren. Zoos, constituting only 2 percent of museums in the United States, served more than 5.5 million schoolchildren, or 12 percent of the total. Art museums, constituting 15 percent, served almost the same number of schoolchildren as zoos. The median zoo served 46,575 schoolchildren; the median aquarium served 24,585.

Large museums of all types, although constituting only 7 percent of the total number of museums, served the largest number of schoolchildren—19 million, or 39 percent of those served. Government-run museums, constituting 41 percent of museums, served just about the same percentage. While federal museums served a disproportionately large number of individuals and had a disproportionately large number of total visits, this pattern does not hold for schoolchildren. State museums served both the largest number and percentage of schoolchildren—6.5 million, or 14 percent—while constituting only 11 percent of the total number of museums.

To enhance the impact of school visits and programs for children, in 1988 more than 1,800 museums offered teacher orientation and training on how to use museum resources. Nearly two-thirds of aquariums and children's museums offered teacher training programs that year.

Number of Exhibitions

American museums produced 49,000 exhibitions in 1988. This figure represents a steady increase over the previous three years, up from 40,000 in 1986 and 44,000 in 1987, for a 23 percent increase.

Exhibitions can take a variety of forms. For a historic house or site, the renovation of an entire room or area is considered the equivalent of an exhibition; for a zoo or aquarium, arboretum or botanical garden, the renovation of a collection area is the equivalent. Some exhibitions are installed in a single location, while others are organized to be toured to several sites, including not only museums but community organizations, schools, public spaces, corporations, and shopping malls. Some exhibitions tour nationally and internationally.

The median art museum produced nine exhibitions in 1988, up from eight in 1986. The median history museum produced five in both years. The median historic site, with less structural flexibility than other museum types, produced three exhibitions a year in the period surveyed. The median aquarium and median zoo, museum types with large investments in permanent installations, had three and two exhibitions, respectively.

Of all the exhibitions produced in 1988, more than one-quarter were permanent, that is, intended to remain on view more than two years. More than half were temporary exhibitions originated and installed by a single museum. About 15 percent of temporary exhibitions traveled to additional sites or were designed to travel only.

Zoos, which on average produce a small number of new exhibitions annually, produced the highest percentage of permanent exhibitions—75 percent. More than half of the exhibitions produced by arboretums and botanical gardens, science museums and technology centers, and aquariums also were permanent. Less than half of the exhibitions produced by other types of museums were permanent, and for art museums the percentage was extremely low, less than 5 percent. The median planetarium had the highest number of permanent exhibitions—five—while the median for most other museum types fell at two.

Conversely, art museums produced more temporary exhibitions than any other museum type. Four-fifths of art museum exhibitions are temporary but do not travel. History museums are the most active in producing traveling exhibitions, with one in five traveling. History museums produced more than 17,000 exhibitions in 1988, but art museums (15 percent of American museums) produced more in proportion to their numbers—nearly 29 percent of the total number of museum exhibitions.

Number of Permanent and Temporary Exhibitions

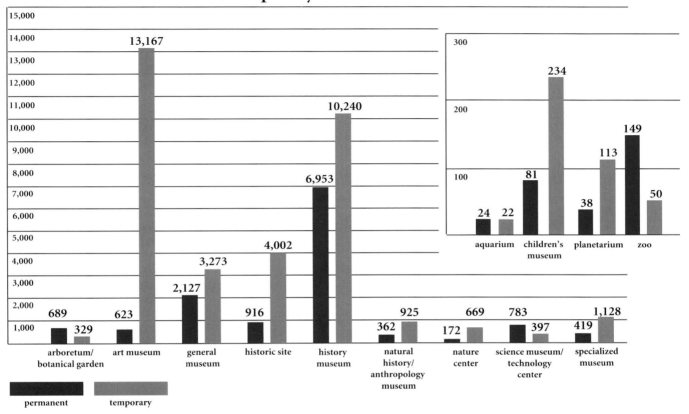

Number of Research Findings Published by Museum Type

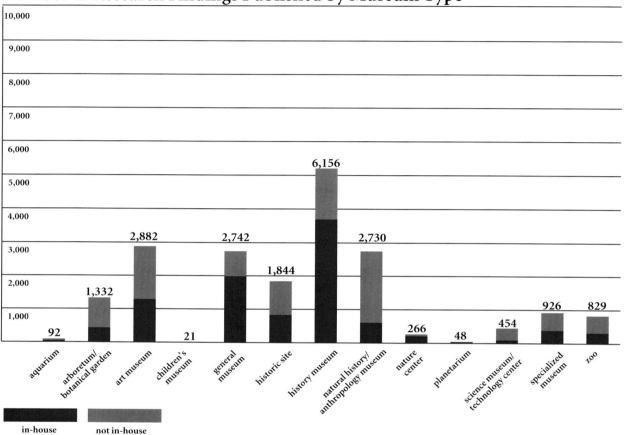

Number of Research Findings Published by Museum Budget Size

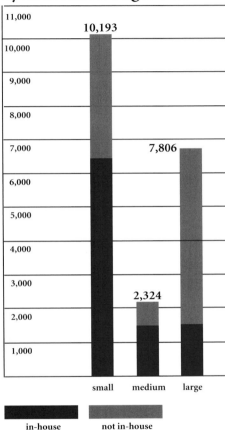

11,000
10,193
10,000
9,000
8,000
7,000
7,806
6,000
5,000
4,000
3,000
2,324
2,000
1,000

small   medium   large

in-house   not in-house

The number of temporary exhibitions museums borrowed or rented from other organizations also shows the highest level of activity among art museums—almost 2,300 exhibitions, about one-third of the total number borrowed or rented in 1988. History museums borrowed or rented nearly one-fifth of that total.

Finally, art and history museums also had the most active loan programs of museum types. In 1988, art museums loaned more than 1,700 exhibitions, and history museums loaned 5,300 exhibitions. Together they accounted for more than two-thirds of exhibitions loaned by U.S. museums in that year—10,300.

Federal museums, although constituting only 7 percent of the total number of museums, loaned 3,400 exhibitions in 1988, while all privately run museums, constituting three-fifths of American museums, together loaned 4,100 exhibitions.

Museums frequently collaborate with other museums or educational institutions in planning, developing, and executing exhibitions. In 1988 more than 3,500 museums reported a formal arrangement with another organization to produce an exhibition. About one-third of these collaborations were with other museums, and one-fifth were with nonmuseum educational institutions. More than 350 of the collaborations were with organizations outside the United States.

Loan and Study

Museum collections and objects loaned for exhibition or study outside the museum are actively serving public purposes. In 1988 museums loaned more than 400,000 objects to other museums and to other institutions in more than 40,000 loan transactions. More than 3,000 museum collections were used in 275,000 visits by outside agencies or individuals for scientific or scholarly research. In the same year more than 20,000 research findings and scholarly or scientific articles related to museum collections were published. More than half of these grew out of studies of the collections of small museums.

6

FACILITIES AND HUMAN RESOURCES

MUSEUM BUILDINGS AND SITES ARE OFTEN LANDMARKS—centers of civic pride, aspects of a regional past preserved, monuments to a community's or state's or nation's sense of itself. Local people made them, and they continue to thrive because local people care about them. Because they are loved by their communities, museums attract the dedication and services of the people to whom they belong. They also attract a work force of specialists committed to the idea and mission of the museum.

Facilities

Taken together, museums in the United States occupy 222 million square feet of interior space. That's equal to nearly 60 Pentagons or 100 Empire State Buildings. They also care for 23 million acres, or nearly 36,000 square miles, equivalent to the state of Indiana.[4]

Most of museums' interior space—71 percent—is owned and operated by privately run museums, while for exterior space the proportion is reversed: 78 percent is owned and managed by government-run museums. The high proportion is explained by the vast natural areas owned and operated by the federal government. In fact, three-quarters of all museum acreage is federal land.

Large museums account for slightly more than half of museums' interior space, while four-fifths of museums' exterior space is in the hands of small museums. The Mountains/Plains region has the largest number of museum acres, 11 million. The Western region has 5.4 million. Of museum types, zoos and aquariums have the largest median interior square footage— 75,500 and 41,000 square feet, respectively. Nature centers have the smallest—3,700 square feet—but at 212 acres, the largest median exterior space.

Museums in the United States occupy

222 million square feet of interior space

. . . they care for 23 million acres, or

nearly 36,000 square miles

Museums allocate a total of 35,126,965 square feet to collections storage. The median art museum has 1,200 square feet of collections storage, while the median historic site has 1,000 square feet, the median history museum has 2,000 square feet, and the median natural history and anthropology museum has 3,000 square feet.

Natural history and anthropology museums, which constitute more than 10 million acres, are responsible for 45 percent of all exterior space under museum control. History museums and historic sites together constitute more than 6 million acres.

Left: Children's Museum of Indianapolis.

Distribution of Interior Square Footage

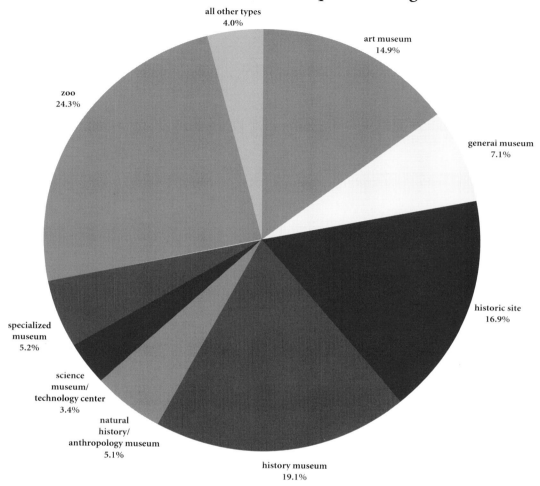

all other types
4.0%

art museum
14.9%

zoo
24.3%

generai museum
7.1%

historic site
16.9%

specialized
museum
5.2%

science
museum/
technology center
3.4%

natural
history/
anthropology museum
5.1%

history museum
19.1%

Note: "all other types" category includes: aquarium 0.6%; arboretum/botanical garden 1.9%; children's museum 0.6%, nature center 0.7%; and planetarium 0.2%.

Distribution of Exterior Acreage

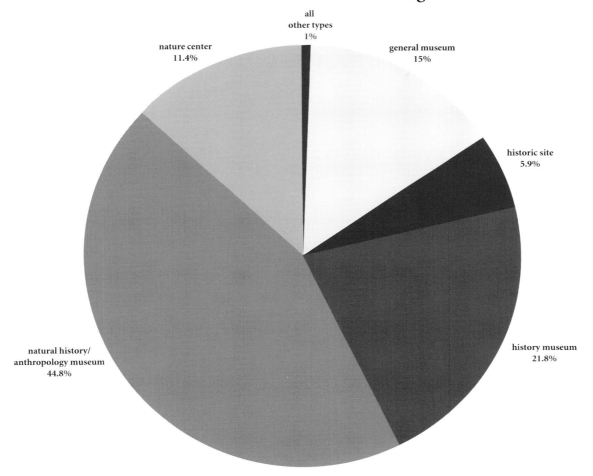

all
other types
1%

general museum
15%

nature center
11.4%

historic site
5.9%

history museum
21.8%

natural history/
anthropology museum
44.8%

Note: "all other types" category includes: aquarium 0.003%; arboretum/botanical garden 0.4%; art museum 0.2%; children's museum 0.01%; planetarium 0.0%; science museum/technology center 0.32%; specialized museum 0.06%; and zoo 0.06%.

Expansion Programs

The 1970s witnessed the largest increase ever in the number of museums founded. This period was followed by a great increase in the number of museums renovating or adding to their buildings and grounds. Almost three-fifths of all museums expanded or undertook what they described as a major renovation in the last 10 years, and 15 percent moved to a new building. Nearly one in three museums added interior square footage, and nearly one in 10 added exterior space. Museums added 33.5 million square feet of interior space and renovated another 20 million square feet. The total museum square footage increased by more than 15 percent. As for exterior space, 841,000 acres were added and more than 1 million acres improved.

This significant expansion of facilities reflects the growing public interest in museums already documented in the continued establishment of new museums and in rising attendance figures. It also reflects museums' need for increased space for expanded exhibition programs, public services, and staff functions, and for new kinds of spaces and facilities to meet higher conservation standards, access requirements for people with disabilities, and innovative presentation strategies such as IMAX films in science museums and habitat immersion exhibits in zoos.

While the aggregate figures portray an expanding field, the median values are sobering: in a 10-year period, one 50 x 50-foot room was added and one 60 x 60-foot room renovated. Even keeping in mind that the median museum has only 8,000 square feet, museum building programs may not be keeping up with needs.

Privately run museums had more active expansion programs than government-run museums. While two-thirds of government-run museums added space, renovated space, and/or moved to new buildings, nearly four-fifths of privately run museums did so. Privately run museums were also more active in acquiring exterior space. Of the museums reporting this type of expansion in the last 10 years, two-thirds were privately run museums. Federal museums, although controlling 76 percent of museums' total exterior space, constituted only 5 percent of museums reporting adding acreage. Of all federal museums, only 7 percent added acreage, an expansion that usually requires congressional approval. Nearly one-fifth of the museums adding acreage during this period were municipal and regional or county museums.

Among types of museums, children's museums had the most active expansion programs. Nearly three-quarters of them undertook major renovations, and two-fifths moved to new locations. Zoos were nearly as active, with three-quarters undertaking major renovations and one-third moving to new locations. Almost half of all science museums moved to new buildings. Planetariums were the least active; only 15 percent undertook renovations.

Percent of Museums by Type Reporting a Major Renovation or Move to a New Building

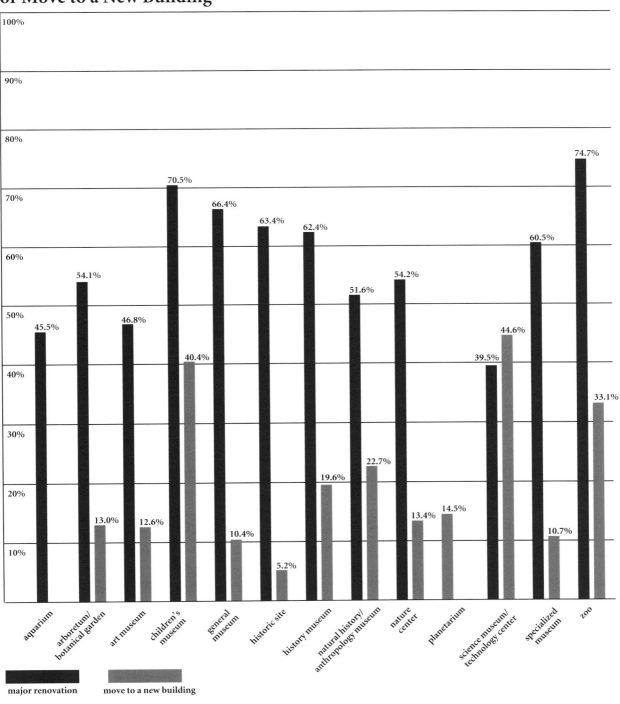

aquarium — major renovation 45.5%

arboretum/botanical garden — major renovation 54.1%, move to a new building 13.0%

art museum — major renovation 46.8%, move to a new building 12.6%

children's museum — major renovation 70.5%, move to a new building 40.4%

general museum — major renovation 66.4%, move to a new building 10.4%

historic site — major renovation 63.4%, move to a new building 5.2%

history museum — major renovation 62.4%, move to a new building 19.6%

natural history/anthropology museum — major renovation 51.6%, move to a new building 22.7%

nature center — major renovation 54.2%, move to a new building 13.4%

planetarium — move to a new building 14.5%

science museum/technology center — major renovation 39.5%, move to a new building 44.6%

specialized museum — major renovation 60.5%, move to a new building 10.7%

zoo — major renovation 74.7%, move to a new building 33.1%

major renovation **move to a new building**

Paid Staff

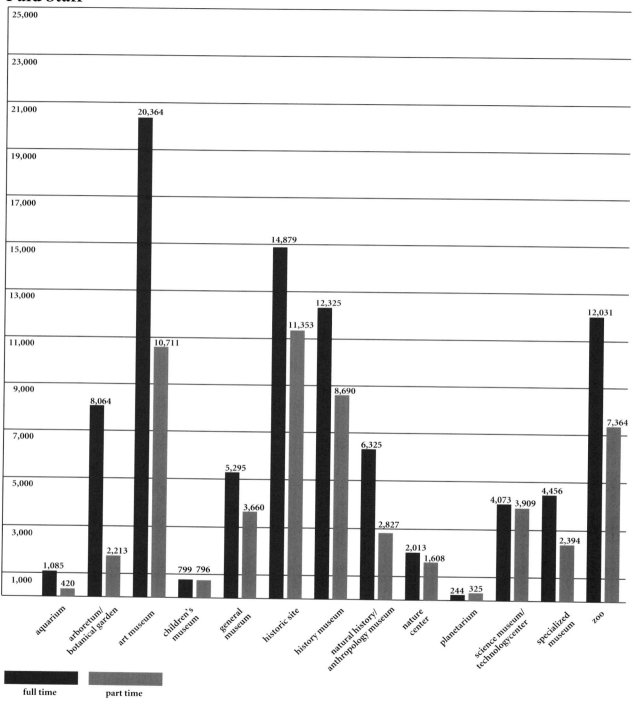

25,000
23,000
21,000
19,000
17,000
15,000
13,000
11,000
9,000
7,000
5,000
3,000
1,000

aquarium — 1,085 | 420
arboretum/botanical garden — 8,064 | 2,213
art museum — 20,364 | 10,711
children's museum — 799 | 796
general museum — 5,295 | 3,660
historic site — 14,879 | 11,353
history museum — 12,325 | 8,690
natural history/anthropology museum — 6,325 | 2,827
nature center — 2,013 | 1,608
planetarium — 244 | 325
science museum/technology center — 4,073 | 3,909
specialized museum — 4,456 | 2,394
zoo — 12,031 | 7,364

■ full time   ▮ part time

Human Resources

The most striking facts about the museum work force are the large number of part-time workers and an astonishing volunteer force, which is more than 2.5 times the size of the total paid staff.

All told, museums employ almost 150,000 people, nearly two-fifths of them part time. The large proportion of part-time personnel reflects the seasonal nature of many museums' staffing needs, particularly nature centers and parks, arboretums and botanical gardens, and outdoor historic sites. College work-study students in university museums and museum interns also generally work part time.

Museums also attract the services of almost 377,000 volunteers. Although nine-tenths of them work part time, some 35,000 volunteers work 35 hours or more per week, essentially a full-time schedule. Of Americans age 18 and older, one in 480 is a museum volunteer.

Art museums, while representing 15 percent of all museums, employ more than 20 percent of the museum work force. Science-related museums, representing another 15 percent of all museums, employ 35 percent of the museum work force. Zoos, nearly one-third of which are classified as large, have the highest average of full-time paid staff. The median zoo employs 65 persons full time. The median history museum (only 2 percent of history museums are classified as large) has a full-time paid staff of three. Conversely, history museums together with historic sites have the most volunteers, nearly 188,000 in all. History museums actually have more full-time volunteers than full-time paid staff. All museum types except planetariums have more part-time volunteers than part-time staff. Planetariums and zoos are the only types of museums with more paid staff, full-time and part-time, than volunteers.

The distribution of paid staff to volunteers by museum type reflects not only differences in the degree of specialization demanded for collections care but also the extent of public programs, as most museum volunteers work with the public. An aquarium, for example, might use docents at information desks only, while a large scientific staff engages in both applied research and science education for young people. A historic site, on the other hand, might have only one full-time staff member to administer the site, care for its artifacts, and direct a dozen volunteers who conduct tours and present school programs. Most museums with active research programs have volunteers behind the scenes, too, assisting curators, scientists, and collections managers.

This large number of volunteers reflects the commitment of Americans to community service and a long history of partnership between volunteers and professionals in the museum world. It is important to remember, too, that most boards of trustees and other types of governing authorities that have the fiduciary responsibility for museums are volunteer entities.

7

FINANCES

MUSEUM SUPPORT HAS ALWAYS BEEN A PUBLIC-PRIVATE PARTNERSHIP. As community institutions, museums receive tax dollars as well as contributions and in-kind donations from the people they serve. All museums, whether private nonprofit organizations or government run, depend on both private and public sectors to meet budgetary needs.

Budgets

In 1988, museums had a total of $4.4 billion in operating income and $4 billion in operating expenses. That's about 2.5 times the size of the two-year budget of the United Nations and exceeds the budgets of 19 individual states. It is about the same as the budget for Oregon. For this figure, operating income is understood to mean unrestricted and restricted funds used for current museum operations such as exhibitions, education, conservation, collections management, research, training, development, public programs, physical facilities maintenance, and administration. Operating expenses is understood to mean expenses for these functions, including in-kind, donated services, and provision of services by an overseeing, or parent, organization.

More than half of American museums have annual incomes of less than $100,000. In 1988 the median operating income for all museums was $86,656. But museum incomes vary dramatically by type. The median operating income for aquariums is $760,000; for zoos, $1,703,627; for general museums, $22,775; and for history museums, $53,266.

The primary sources of museum support demonstrate the public-private partneship. Museums receive nearly one-third of their income from government sources . . . and two-fifths from investments and earned income

Income

Museums derive their income from a variety of sources, including allocations from parent organizations and friends organizations; allocations and grants from federal, state, and local governments; contributions from foundations and corporations; contributions and grants from individuals; receipts from benefits and special events; interest from endowments and similar funds; the occasional sale of assets; and earned income.

The primary sources of museum support demonstrate the public-private partnership. Museums receive nearly one-third of their income from government sources; if indirect government support received through government-funded parent organizations is included, the figure is two-fifths. Another two-fifths of museum income is generated through investments and what is classified as earned income—admission fees, memberships, royalties, publications, tuition and

High Museum of Art, Atlanta.
© 1987 E. Alan McGee.

Sources of Museum Total Operating Income

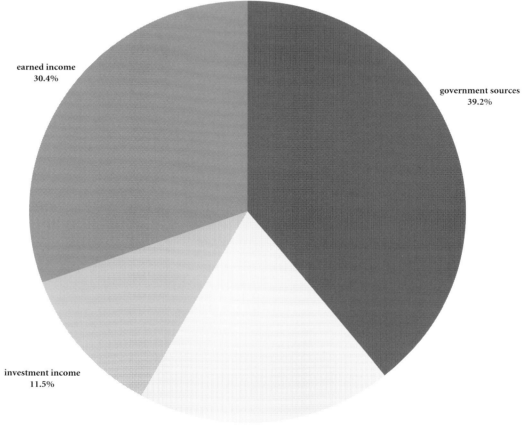

earned income
30.4%

government sources
39.2%

investment income
11.5%

private sources
18.9%

Sources of Operating Income for All Museums, 1979 and 1988

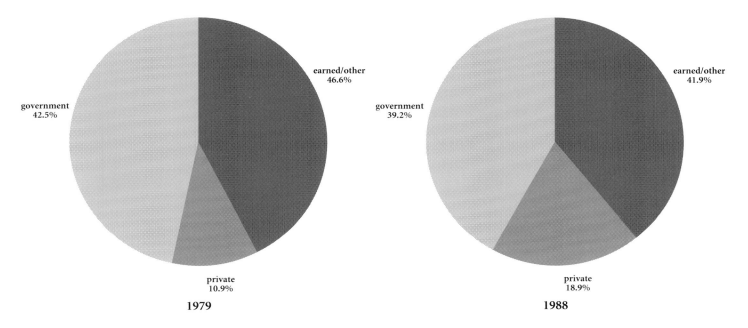

1979

earned/other
46.6%

government
42.5%

private
10.9%

1988

earned/other
41.9%

government
39.2%

private
18.9%

Note: 1979 figures from 1979 Museum Program Survey.

program fees, fees for services to other museums such as the loan of traveling exhibitions or conservation of objects, food services, direct mail sales, museum shop sales, parking, and facilities rental. About one-fifth is from private contributions from foundations, corporations, and individuals.

Overall, the percentage of earned income is down from 1979, as is the percentage of government allocations. Income from private sources is up. The percentage of earned income fell by 5 percentage points; the percentage from government sources fell by 3 percentage points. The percentage of income from private sources nearly doubled, from almost 11 to almost 19 percent. These shifts reflect, in part, reductions in government support to museums during the Reagan administration. While museums in the past two decades have been increasingly innovative in generating earned income, the decline in the proportion from this source may indicate that it has been tapped to its maximum. The increase in income from private sources reflects the increasing aggressiveness of museums in seeking such support, the expansion of development staffs, and changing patterns of private and corporate giving.

In 1988 museums received more than $368 million in direct allocations from parent organizations and friends organizations. They also returned about $108 million to parent organizations. Museums received an estimated $143 million worth of in-kind donations for goods and services from parent organizations—a computer purchased by a university for use in the university museum, for example. Building maintenance and groundskeeping were the services most frequently cited as provided by parent organizations; nearly 5,000 museums received them. Thirty-five percent of museums have a separately incorporated friends group or foundation whose sole purpose is to provide services or raise funds.

Five income sources were documented in the 1989 National Museum Survey: contributions of parent organizations and friends organizations, government sources, private sources, investment income (including endowment income), and earned income. More details for government sources, endowments, and earned income follow.

Government Sources

Museums reported receiving $1.2 billion from government sources in 1988.[5] This figure does not include indirect government support received through parent organizations. Of all government allocations, general museums received the largest share—$312 million. This figure is influenced by the fact that all Smithsonian museums, for the purposes of this survey, were classified as general museums. Art museums received the next largest share—$212 million, or 17 percent of government's allocation to museums. In fact, when figures for the Smithsonian are excluded, art museums received the largest share of government and all other income sources documented in the survey. Taken together, science-related museums received $343 million, or one-quarter of gover ment allocations. The smallest share of government allocations (amounting to $4.7 million) went to planetariums.

Museums report a range of from $75 to $218,357,000 in income from government sources, with a median of $22,300. The median for large museums is $84,050; for medium-sized museums, $51,849; and for small museums, $5,100.

Of museum types, the median government allocation is highest for science museums and technology centers ($157,336) and aquariums ($156,000) and smallest for historic sites and history museums (each $7,000). Of regions, the medians are highest for the Mountain/ Plains ($60,000) and Mid-Atlantic ($58,600) and lowest for the Midwest ($7,500).

Allocations from state governments totaled $244.7 million, and from local governments, $413.3 million. Of the total government allocations to museums in 1988, 41 percent was from the federal government, 20 percent from state governments, and 34 percent from local governments; 5 percent was from other government sources.

Endowments

In 1988 museums reported a total of $427 million in investment income, constituting 12 percent of all income. Of this, 13 percent is endowment income. One-half of American museums have endowments. Three-quarters of large museums have endowments, while only 45 percent of small museums have them. Sixty-three percent of privately run museums have endowments, while only 28 percent of government-run museums have them. Sixty-one percent of children's museums and history museums have endowments.

The total value of museum endowments is $14 billion. Ninety-three percent of this total is held by large museums. Art museums have by far the largest endowments, totaling $10.6 billion, or 76 percent of all museum endowment value. Privately run museums also have by far the largest share (96 percent) of endowment value.

The median endowment for all museums is $125,000. Median figures range from $7.2 million for aquariums, to $5 million for planetariums, to $90,000 for children's museums.

More than 1,500 museums have a policy regarding how much of the earnings from endowments will be used and how much will be reinvested. This policy is sometimes approved by the governing authority, sometimes created by the staff.

Planned-giving programs are a relatively new effort by museums to build endowments. These programs involve the active solicitation of charitable gifts that come through wills, trusts, gift annuities, life insurance, securities, and real estate. In 1988 nearly 1,500 museums had such a program in place, and more than 1,100 were developing one. As a group, more large museums have planned-giving programs than small museums.

Percent of Museums with Endowments by Type

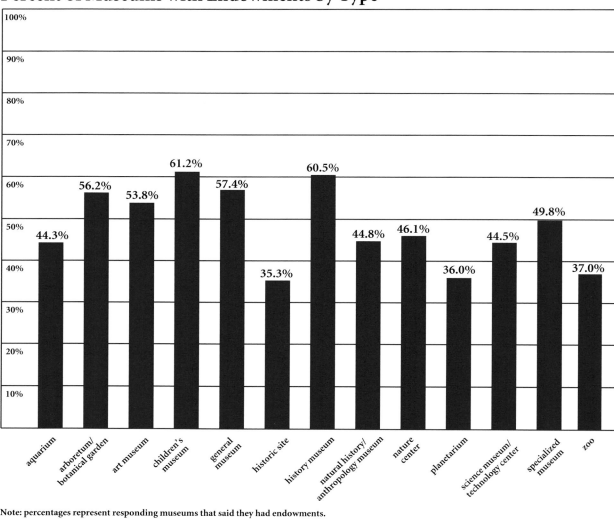

Note: percentages represent responding museums that said they had endowments.

Earned Income

In 1988 museums reported $1.1 billion in earned income. Art museums reported the highest total—$290 million, or about 28 percent of all their income. While overall earned income constituted about 30 percent of museum income, for aquariums it constituted 73 percent. Zoos had the second highest aggregate earned income—$249 million. Planetariums, a museum type of which there are only a small number in the United States, had the smallest aggregate earned income in 1988—$6.5 million. The median operating income for a small planetarium that year was $60,000; for a large planetarium, $3,463,318.

Admission fees constitute one element of earned income. In 1988, museums received a total of $570 million from this source. Most museums—55 percent—charge admission, either a fixed fee or a suggested donation at the door. The median admission fee for a nonmember adult is $2, and for a nonmember child, $1, although there is considerable variation in fees by museum type and governing authority. Arboretums and botanical gardens have the highest median fixed admission fee for nonmember adults—$4. General museums, at $1.50, have the lowest.

More than 80 percent of zoos and children's museums have entry fees, while only 36 percent of art museums and 40 percent of nature centers have them. Sixty percent of privately run museums charge fees, while 48 percent of government-run museums do so; of these, 63 percent of state museums charge fees. At the other end of the spectrum are museums associated with public schools and colleges, only 28 percent of which charge admission.

There is clearly a trend toward charging admission. The 1979 IMS survey reported that only 32 percent of museums charged admission, while in 1988, 55 percent did so. Many museums that charge entrance fees continue to have regular or occasional free days, and museum public relations staffs like to point out that a museum visit is usually cheaper than a movie.

Museum membership programs are another source of earned income. More than 4,000 museums had such a program in 1988. Privately run museums as a group have nearly three times as many membership programs as government-run museums, and large museums as a group have more membership programs than small museums.

Museums have nearly 9 million members; on average, one American in 28 is a museum member. The Smithsonian Institution alone has more than 2.5 million members. The median membership fee for all museums is $15 a year for individuals and $25 for families. History museums and historic sites have the lowest median membership fees—$10 for individuals and $15 for families. Art museums and planetariums have the highest—$25 for individuals and $30 for families. Fees for large museums ($25 and $35) are higher than for small museums ($15 and $25).

Percent of Museums Charging Admission Fees

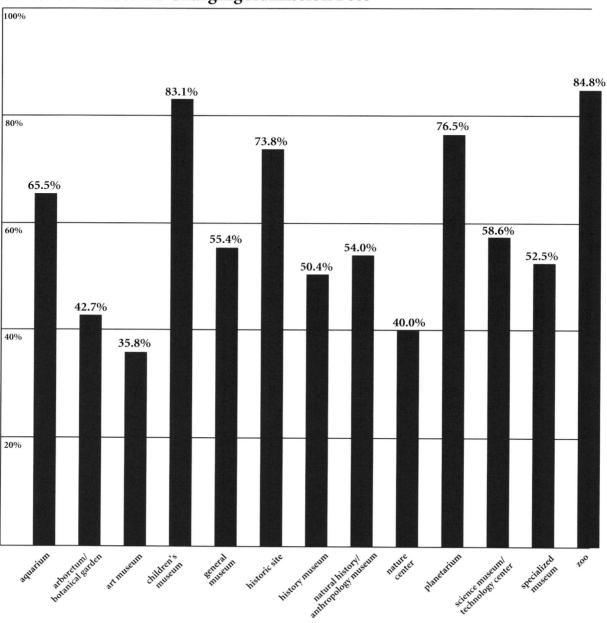

Percent of Museums Charging Admission Fees, 1979 and 1988

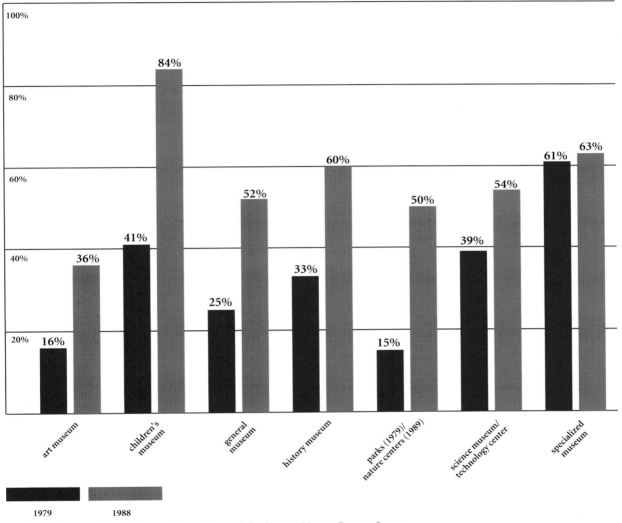

1979 figures from 1979 Museum Program Survey. Types as defined in 1979 Museum Program Survey.

Number of Museums by Operating Expenses

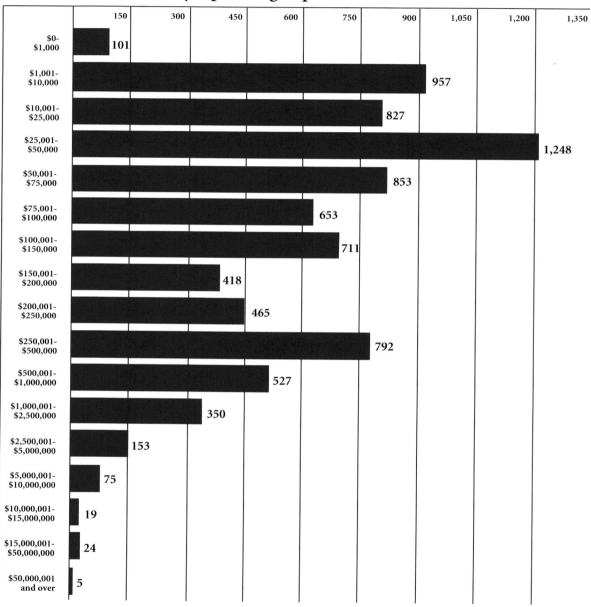

Operating Expenses	Number of Museums
$0-$1,000	101
$1,001-$10,000	957
$10,001-$25,000	827
$25,001-$50,000	1,248
$50,001-$75,000	853
$75,001-$100,000	653
$100,001-$150,000	711
$150,001-$200,000	418
$200,001-$250,000	465
$250,001-$500,000	792
$500,001-$1,000,000	527
$1,000,001-$2,500,000	350
$2,500,001-$5,000,000	153
$5,000,001-$10,000,000	75
$10,000,001-$15,000,000	19
$15,000,001-$50,000,000	24
$50,000,001 and over	5

Slightly more than half the museums charging admission offer a discount for members. Nearly three-quarters of the privately run museums that charge admission offer member discounts, while only about one-quarter of government-run museums do so.

Operating Expenses

Art museums have the largest aggregate budgets among museums. Although constituting only 15 percent of the total number of museums in the United States, they account for the largest share of operating expenses—28 percent. The median art museum has operating expenses of $163,761. Zoos (2 percent of all museums) account for the next largest share, 12 percent. Zoos are, in fact, the most expensive type of museum to operate, with the median operating expenses at $1,233,628. Aquariums have a median of $546,158, history museums, $50,000. In considering varying budget sizes by museum types, it is important to recall the differing demands among museum disciplines and the varying distribution of museum types among the categories small, medium, and large (see p. 21).

Museum Personnel Expenses by Type

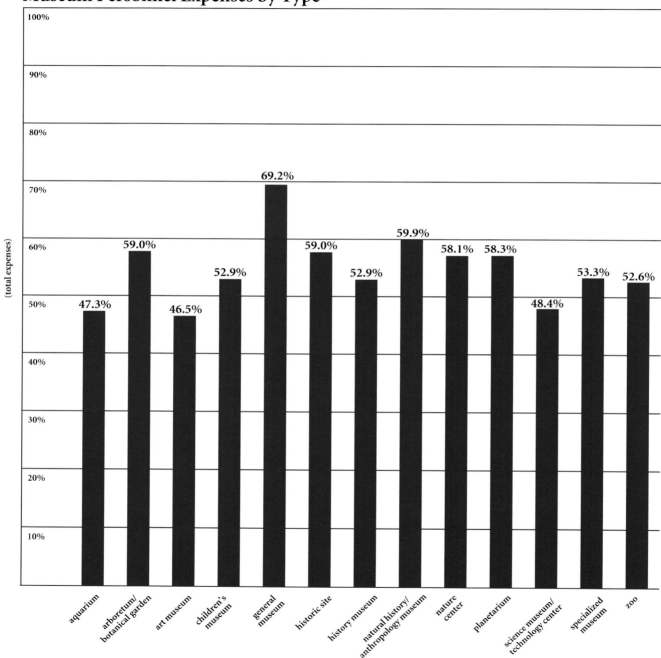

(total expenses)

- 100%
- 90%
- 80%
- 70%
- 60%
- 50%
- 40%
- 30%
- 20%
- 10%

Type	Percentage
aquarium	47.3%
arboretum/botanical garden	59.0%
art museum	46.5%
children's museum	52.9%
general museum	69.2%
historic site	59.0%
history museum	52.9%
natural history/anthropology museum	59.9%
nature center	58.1%
planetarium	58.3%
science museum/technology center	48.4%
specialized museum	53.3%
zoo	52.6%

Personnel Expenses

Personnel expenses account for the largest share of museum operating expenses—54 percent. Art museums, which account for 28 percent of total museum operating expenses, incur 24 percent of total personnel expenses. Personnel expenses account for 47 percent of operating expenses in art museums, while for natural history and anthropology museums they constitute 60 percent. Generally, the larger the museum budget, the smaller the proportion allocated to personnel expenses. For history museums and historic sites, however, nine-tenths of which are small, personnel expenses average almost 56 percent of operating budgets, slightly more than the average for all museums.

In some museums, parent organizations and friends organizations pay personnel salaries. Of full-time staff, three-quarters are paid by the museum, but only slightly over two-fifths of part-time staff are paid by the museum. When temporary or seasonal staff are added to part-time staff, the portion paid by the museum rises to 81 percent. Parent and friends organizations pay for almost 19 percent of part-time staff.

Among other functions, collections and research expenses and public activities have the largest museum budget allocations, each constituting nearly one-quarter of total budgets.

NOTES

1. Medians are sometimes given instead of averages as they correct for disproportions introduced by large museums. Because of rounding, percents may not add up to 100. Because percents were calculated on raw data and numbers on weighted data, discrepancies within profiles may exist.

2. The median income of general museums, at $22,775 (also appears on page 34), reflects the small size of the sample and thus the statistical significance of each museum responding. Specifically, if the lowest two surveys are omitted from the results (the lowest reports a gross annual income of $28), then, because of the way statistical weighting operates, the median budget for small museums moves from $22,775, which seems too low, to $60,000, which seems about right. Similarly, removing the highest two surveys (the highest is $474 million, the second highest $54 million) reduces the average from $1.9 million to $763,000.

3. While it is statistically true that there are no planetariums in the Mountain/Plains region, the 1988 *Official Museum Directory* lists nine planetariums, observatories, and astronomy museums in the region for that year. There is no way to know if these institutions are planetariums or are museums as defined in the survey. Some planetariums may have listed themselves as science museums in the survey. Moreover, while the sample taken as a whole has statistical validity, individual data elements—particularly for the smaller classes of museums or for secondary attributes such as geographic distribution—have less statistical validity than the whole. Similar anomalies occur, for example, with figures for aquariums.

4. If the top three largest acreage amounts are removed—1.5, 1.4, and 1.2 million acres, with the fourth largest response being 396,000 acres—then because of the way the weighting acts on the numbers, the total drops to 9.3 million acres, or closer to Connecticut, Massachusetts, and Rhode Island combined.

5. The $1.2 billion is from a figure of $3.7 billion for total museum income, a figure lower than the total museum income reported ($4.4 billion) because some museums did not respond to the question asking them to break income out by source. Different rates of response for different portions of the survey resulted in expected variation.

Charts and graphs are based on the *Data Report from the 1989 National Museum Survey* and on the larger survey database. Because of rounding, pie charts may add up to slightly more or less than 100 percent. Because of partial responses, totals may differ from graph to graph. Variations in methods of figuring percentages off weighted values produce additional small discrepancies. See the *Data Report* for full explanations of the statistical method.

REFERENCES

American Association of Museums. *Data Report from the 1989 National Museum Survey*. Washington, D.C.: American Association of Museums, January 1992.

———. *The Official Museum Directory, 1988*. Wilmette, Ill.: National Register Publishing Co., 1987.

Commission on Museums for a New Century. *Museums for a New Century*. Washington, D.C.: American Association of Museums, 1984.

Kimche, Lee. "American Museums: The Vital Statistics," *Museum News*, October 1980, pp. 52–57.

Price, Lewis C., Lisa DiRocco, and Janice D. Lewis. *Museum Program Survey, 1979*. Washington, D.C.: National Center for Education Statistics, March 1981. The Institute of Museum Services' 1979 survey of museums.

U.S. Bureau of the Census. *State Population and Household Estimates: July 1, 1989*. Washington, D.C.: Department of Commerce, March 1990.

———. *Statistical Abstract of the United States, 1990*. Washington, D.C.: Government Printing Office, 1990.

The World Almanac and Book of Facts, 1989. New York: World Almanac, 1988.

INDEX

Volunteers: 24, 81
  as members of board of directors: 39
  as part-time workers: 81
  as percentage of paid staff: 81
  as staff in all museums: 40, 81
  as staff in aquariums: 41
  as staff in arboretums and botanical
    gardens: 42
  as staff in art museums: 43, 81
  as staff in children's museums: 44, 81
  as staff in general museums: 45, 81
  as staff in historic sites: 46, 81
  as staff in history museums: 47, 81
  as staff in natural history and anthro-
    pology museums: 48, 81
  as staff in nature centers: 49, 81
  as staff in planetariums: 50, 81
  as staff in science museums and tech-
    nology centers: 51, 81
  as staff in specialized museums: 52, 81
  as staff in zoos: 53, 81
  full-time workers: 50
  numbers of: 81
  part-time workers: 81
  in research: 81

W
Weeks open to public: 24
Western region
  acreage for museums: 75
  all museums: 27, 33, 40
  aquariums: 41
  arboretums and botanical gardens: 42
  art museums: 43
  children's museums: 44
  general museums: 45
  historic sites: 46
  history museums: 47
  natural history and anthropology
    museums: 27, 48
  nature centers: 49
  planetariums: 50
  science museums: 51
  specialized museums: 52
  zoos: 53
Williams, Patricia E.: 13
Wint, Dennis: 13
Workforce. *See* Staff; Volunteers
Workshops: 61

Y
6/27

Youth museums. *See* Children's museums

Z
Zoos
  admission fees: 53, 89
  age of: 33
  attendance: 53, 63
  earned income: 89
  endowments: 53
  establishment date: 53
  exhibitions: 53
  facilities expansion: 78
  governance: 53
  habitat: 78
  interior square footage: 53, 75
  major renovations: 78
  number of: 53
  number of sites: 53
  oldest museum type: 23
  operating expenses: 53, 93
  operating income: 53, 83
  permanent exhibitions: 53
  profile: 53
  regional distribution: 53
  renovations: 78
  school children served: 53
  size distribution: 53
  staff: 53, 81
  volunteers: 53, 81